Raising Children of Alcoholics & Drug Users

By Joan Callander Dingle and Chad Dingle

Raising Children of Alcoholics & Drug Users

www.AddictsKids.com

Published by WordGatherers Publishing LLC
West Linn, Oregon 97068
ISBN 978-0-945272-59-5

Cover and interior design by:
Dennis Marcellino
www.LighthousePublishingCo.com/marcellinodesign/bookdesign.html

Library of Congress Control Number: 2015909567

Contents

Introduction & Our Story   7

Part One: Addictions

1. Coming to Terms   16
2. Helping Kids Beat the Odds   26

Part Two: Legal

3. Handling the Legal Stuff Part One: Adoption, Guardianship, Custody & Related Matters   34
4. Handling the Legal Stuff Part Two: Wills, Estates, and Family Talks   49

Part Three: Visitations

5. The Reality of Visitations   60
6. Behind Bars Visitations   76
7. 'Heart Smart' Holidays   86

Part Four: Words & Feelings

8. Words Matter: A Message for Parenting Grandparents   97
9. Counseling   107
10. Emotions Don't Need a Label...or Do They?   122
11. Difficult Questions, Powerful Answers   129

Part Five: Schools & Parenting

12. Family Trees & Other School Landmines — 141

13. Parenting Children with Special Needs & Challenging Behaviors — 148

14. Teens: Technology, Sex and Other Things that Drive Parents Crazy — 163

15. When Children of Addicts Grow Up — 176

Part Six: Help Guide

Resource Appendix — 183

Footnotes — 189

Index — 198

Losing Family Obliges Us to Find Our family.

Mike Rich, Finding Forester

Introduction & Our Story

The term functioning addict is an oxymoron. Some argue that mothers or fathers, who overindulge in drinking, or use drugs, can parent adequately. However, since your loved one's life is falling apart or shattered, and their kids are hurting, you know that isn't true. *Numerous books try to help people get sober or stay clean. Other books facilitate reuniting families. Our book doesn't do either. Instead, we focus on the problems, needs and emotions of children of addicts and those who parent them.* Practical advice, information, options, opportunities and solutions are taken from our own experience, professionals and courageous individuals who openly talk about their own heartaches and triumphs.

Children can't wait for their birthparent to get sober, and against the odds, stay sober. *Every day, every phase in a child's life is critical. What happens in childhood is the foundation for the rest of their life.* Toddler or teen, young people need a safe, stable, loving home life with boundaries and supervision; and they need it now. They need you to be there for them no matter what. They need you to stand up for them in court, school, against their using parent, and throughout their life.

"We can start by recognizing every kid's need for a family who can provide the normal experiences of eating at the family table and playing after-school sports. A family who can be there when a child learns to read and gets a driver's license, and who is still there — in ways we all know are important — when he graduates from college, gets his first job, marries and has children of his own."[1] This, or a reasonable variation of, is what normal looks like in a healthy family and this is what you, not an addict or alcoholic, provides.

Years ago, I adopted my now twenty three-year-old grandson, Chad, and together we are writing this book. Our story isn't unique and it isn't important, except to reassure you that we understand much of what you are facing and feeling. What we share in this chapter, and throughout the book, are short pieces from a very long and ugly saga. My daughter, Brandy (who I also adopted), is Chad's birth mother. I divorced the only father she knew after she graduated from high school. Big mistake. It rocked her world, and she turned to the wrong crowd in college looking for love, but instead found trouble. Within a year she was pregnant with Chad. She has spent the last twenty-five years drifting between drugs, alcohol, and unhealthy relationships. His birth father, Donald, had problems with alcohol and anger. It was only a few months ago that Donald contacted Chad and apologized for 'not being there' for him. Sorry, but it was a lot more than 'not being there'…he was a danger to Chad when he was 'there', and so was my daughter. But I respect the courage it took for him to reach out when he did, and his restraint in not doing so when Chad turned eighteen and was still discovering who he was, and what he was capable of achieving.

My birthparents never married and weren't together when I was born, or later. Their choices forever changed my life—and the lives of many others. What we're writing is the hardcore truth; it's not sugar coated or exaggerated. I know what I went through and how hard it was, and I want you to understand, and overcome, your own personal struggles easier than I did. The little notes and memorabilia that my mom kept over the years show the journey that I went through to get to where I am now.[2]

Our story

Chad lived with Brandy in smoke-filled apartments, littered with animal feces and other filth, from the time he was tiny until he was two when Oregon Child Protective Services placed him in foster care after neighbors reported seeing massive bruising on him. Later, I learned that the bruises were because he was intermittently spanked on his buttocks and feet for four hours for refusing to eat.

Brandy and her two gay male roommates, who she babysat for in exchange for room and board, were arrested. I moved Brandy back home with me after her release on bail. She enrolled in cosmetology school, staying clean until her trial six months later. A family friend gave her a part time job in his law office, and defended her in court. During the six months of waiting, the young men pleaded guilty to criminal charges and then tragically committed suicide rather than face jail or being separated from each other. Tragically, their kids went back to a drug-using mother—the devastation around addicts and alcoholics never stops. Unless you break free your life will constantly mirror theirs—filled with drama and trauma. Brandy was given a huge chance to turn her life around when, due to their death of the only eyewitnesses, the multiple felony charges against her were reduced to a single misdemeanor and she was given probation. She blew the chance by moving in, even before her sentencing, with a drug dealer who was on parole for armed robber, which of course she never mentioned. I immediately called Child Services and tried to get custody of Chad. State workers were initially skeptical that my priorities had changed, and that Chad's safety and interests were, and would remain, my top priority. They eventually relented after my aging parents intervened by personally going into the local office and talking with the branch director. Within a couple of days Chad left the care of strangers and moved in with me. I talked by phone with Brandy, and she visited Chad occasionally, until she and the dealer were arrested for being in possession of a controlled substance. Brandy was jailed while waiting for her hearing, and ended up in prison for violating her probation. By my choice, we had no contact.

Within a few weeks of being released from prison, Brandy married another drug user, Ryan, who I had never met. *I only discovered the truth about Ryan's addiction years later...I was very naïve and foolishly believed my daughter's lies for years or I would have done things much differently from the very beginning.* Their three daughters, Chad's half sisters, have been shuffled between them and other people ever since. One parent and then the other, sometimes both at the same time, have cycled up and down. Their daughter's lives have been hell, but I am getting ahead of our story.

Chad lived with me for about a year and then the caseworker placed him with his birth dad, Donald, who had demanded custody once the state of Oregon began garnishing his wages for back child-support. It was well documented that Donald had drinking and anger problems, but state workers thought his attending mandated parenting and anger control classes would correct the problems. They were wrong, and it didn't take a crystal ball to predict the outcome. I hired an attorney and obtained legal standing as Chad's psychological parent. I also requested, and was granted, visitation rights. Chad stayed with me one weekend a month and alternating holidays. By the second visit, he was telling me how his dad slapped him, and how he was scared when he couldn't wake Donald some mornings. He'd beg me not to drink. I seldom drank alcohol and never when he was with me, but I quickly realized that any can or beverage bottle panicked him.

I repeatedly called the caseworker and relayed what Chad said, and did, but she claimed that she couldn't do anything unless there were physical signs of abuse. *Normally it is policy, not social workers, creating roadblocks; however, taking no chances when Chad showed up with metal spatula abrasions on his bottom and legs the eighth month, I called the police.* We never went back to Donald's apartment—even for his things. Together we faced years of counseling, and continuing family problems. I handled the legal battles on my own—shielding Chad the best I could.

Author notes

Chad writes as a child of *two* users. He was so traumatized after living with Donald, that at age of four, he was diagnosed with Post Traumatic Stress Syndrome, back when the term was unknown to the average person. I write as the mother of *one user.* I was so sheltered that I didn't know anyone who used drugs, or had been arrested—certainly no one who had their children removed from their custody. I wrote my first book *Second Time Around: Help for Parents Who Raise Their Children's Kids* because, at that time, there were no books on the subject and no one talked about the growing drug problem. I now know a lot that I wish I wouldn't have had to learn—you will go through a tsunami of pain—but you will make it.

Life is a series of options and opportunities, and with addicts and alcoholics the choices you face suck. If you feel like you're on a dark roller coaster ride controlled by a son, daughter, spouse, or 'ex' then get off and take control. You can't always choose your circumstances, but you can choose your attitude, and you can look for alternatives that move you to a better place in your life.
One of your first choices is deciding to go it alone if you are a mom or dad, or to take over parenting if you are a grandparent or other relative. *One of the toughest choices is* determining

what, if any, roles the addict or alcoholic should play in yours, and their children's, future. *Trying to avoid hurting the addict only enables them, and risks destroying the rest of your family.* At some point you'll probably end up having to tell the user that you are saving their children from them—not for them. Be just as open, but in incremental and in age-appropriate terms, when answering kids' questions, and in discussing their parents.

For most of my life mom kept Brandy away, and chose how much interaction we had. But when I got older, it was my choice. We never let Brandy have an option and that was how it needed to be. As mom said, you aren't saving the child for the addict; you're doing it for the child.

Chad amazes me. As a freshman, he started cutting and threatened suicide because Brandy broke her promise to him to never use again. The depth of his memories and feelings no longer wound my heart because Chad has moved beyond them. He is rock solid in who he is, and who he wants in his life. It took years of counseling, hurting, and living to get through the aftershocks of his experiences. There were times when I cried so hard that I was sick to my stomach, or I slept on the floor too exhausted to pull myself up and get into bed. There were times when Chad yelled the most hateful things at me, and slammed his fist through walls in anger. It's been a grueling journey, but life now is normal and good. Chad and I are thankful for many things: Brandy did not get an abortion, his genes and life experiences make him who he is today, our faith is an integral part of who we are, and I gained a son.

The love factor

When Chad and I first talked about writing a book, he suggested 'Love or Addiction' for the title, "because it summarizes everything...you can't have both." I disagreed. I think it's the combination of 'Love and Addiction' that clouds your judgment, and shreds your heart. Although we ultimately chose another title, we realized that '*and/or*' are important and defining differences. Understanding these differences will help you parent, and help you work through conflicting emotions.

Love is an emotion that cannot be defined. It's irrational and incomprehensible. I like to say that loving someone means that you are willing to do anything for that person. Many people use the idea of taking a bullet for someone, however to me, that is a "one moment" thing. Love is a hard journey and it takes work. My best metaphor is that of a sinking ship. If you love someone, you could follow the hard journey all the way to the end and stay on the ship, even if it's sinking, but sometimes you have to get off. When it came to Brandy, both my mom and I had to get off. She may have been family by blood, but blood doesn't mean family.

I knew and loved Brandy before drugs. I drove home from the hospital with her in my arms, and watched her on the soccer field with a broken nose pleading to play. I remember her first dance, the misfits she protected from bullies, and a kaleidoscope of birthdays, summer camps, and kisses. Brandy was the center of my heart for over twenty years.

Chad's few happy memories with Brandy were lost long ago. He never cried for his mommy from the first day he came to live with me, but was happy to see her in those early years. Later, even as I kept creating opportunities for the two of them to be together, he displayed mixed feelings. Still later there was all the "Who am I issues?" that all adolescents—but especially those who are adopted—go through. I thought it was safe to have Brandy in his life because I was there for visits and believed I understood their relationship. By the time I found out how wrong I was, Chad was devastated and suicidal.

Unknown to me, they talked often on the phone at night and had bonded.

Brandy is my birth mother, not my mom. We have had our good times and bad; ultimately it has ended up that I don't remember her doing drugs. I don't remember living with her at all. For a while I did like knowing where she was because I wanted to know that she was okay. However, now I want to know where she is so that I don't ever see her. She caused me a lot of pain, even as an adult. That pain doesn't end with me, but extends to the people around me, including Jessica, my wife. And when it comes to that, I don't want her around anymore.

Chad had horrific memories of his birth dad. For example, a year after his return Chad told me that one morning when he woke up that Donald was gone and there were four strangers in their apartment. He said three of the men soon left, and as he was telling me Chad crawled off the kitchen barstool and cowered under the kitchen counter. No amount of coaxing could get him to continue the story. Similar fragmented 'glimpses' continued surfacing through late high school when counseling helped him through the remaining blockages.

I too have bad memories of Donald, including his asking how much it was worth to me for him to get out of Chad's and my lives. I would have paid anything, but only to attorneys and counselors, not to Donald. Still, I understand the blood bond for Chad is there. I also respect the probability that Donald did change, and does have regrets. Chad is slowly getting to know Donald, and his extended birth family, adding another twist to "love and/or addiction."

The twist is that for a child acceptance from a parent, no matter how much pain they caused, is important. I can't compare my relationship with Brandy to that of

Donald. I can't apply the "love and/or addiction" for my birth father because I can only use what I feel and remember about him, and until recently, that was hate. I just wanted him to see the person I'd become, see what he missed, and to let him know that I forgive him. Over time I learned from counselors to forgive the ones that hurt me. It's hard, but I forgave Brandy for the early years, and Donald for everything. It makes things a lot easier. When you realize that you don't always have to hate them, it takes a big burden off your life.

'Tough love' doesn't begin to describe the emotions, or choices, facing you. It takes courage. Not all love stories are Hallmark showpieces. *Sometimes the simple journey of hanging on one more day, making it through one more night, is the love story.*

I didn't cause it. I can't cure it.
I can't control it. I can care for myself...

National Association for Children of Alcoholics

1
Coming to Terms

I didn't cause it

"I didn't cause their addiction." Say it out loud. Put it on a sticky note and tape it to your mirror. Make it your screen saver. Do whatever it takes until you believe it in your mind, and accept it in your heart.

Users want you to think that they drink, or take drugs, because you are not a good parent or partner. Don't buy into it. They use chemicals to blur a reality they don't like, mask physical or emotional pain, or because they like the party life. It works temporarily but doesn't solve underlying issues. Addicts get caught up in a need to indulge more frequently, or keep increasing the dosage, in order to maintain their original high. This creates more problems and more serious consequences. While they didn't smoke their first joint, swallow their first pain pill after surgery, or down their first beer knowing they would get hooked, they will self-destruct if they don't stop.

Some users play the heredity card, "Grandpa was an alcoholic—it's in my blood." I don't think so. "Genes provide only probabilistic

propensities, not predetermined programming. They provide prob-
abilities for behavior and risk factors for disease [addiction] but do
not indicate whether any individual will sustain a behavior or suc-
cumb to a particular mental or physical disorder..."3

*Many substance abusers complain that life is unfair. They are
right, nothing new there. Life is unfair; but life is equally
unfair to everyone, just in different ways.* Some kids have a
mom who commits suicide; others have a dad fighting in a war,
or they were born without legs. Bullying happens to smaller
framed boys and larger girls. A company downsizes and hard-
working people lose their job. It doesn't matter what today's
circumstances, or yesterday's experiences bring, *everyone has
to learn how to deal with problems rather than run from them,
or numb themself through substance abuse in order to survive.*

Addicts (term used interchangeably with alcoholics throughout
the book) will also tell their young sons or daughters that it is
your fault, or worse, their fault. "I wouldn't drink so much if
your mother had a better paying job or if you did your homework." These messages are toxic. They burrow into children's minds. It takes lots of conversations and reassurances to
override their negative effect.

**A lot of people think that children don't "understand"
what a parent is saying to them, but the reality is that
they do. In fact, what they've been told can surface as
dreams sometimes and then those dreams become memories that can cause a lifetime of pain. An addict should
never blame someone else for their problem; it is their
problem and theirs alone. No one else made them start,
and no one else has the power to stop them.**

I can't cure it

Chad and I aren't qualified, and couldn't debate if wanted to,
whether addiction is a disease, genetic predisposition, culturally

induced, or something else history has yet to reveal. The 'why' doesn't matter to a one-month-old crying because he is hungry, or a five-year-old whose mom promised to show up for Thanksgiving, and didn't. It doesn't stop a teenager's embarrassment, or fear, as their parent is hauled away in a police car and they are being driven to a foster home, or left to fend for themselves.

The tentacles of drugs are incredibly strong. They attack the whole body including teeth, heart, and liver while also altering cognitive and emotional brain processes. It starts the first time meth is used. [4] *Methamphetamine "carries a prognosis worse than many cancers,"[5] "very few people can quit...[there is a] very high death rate,"* says Michael Sise M.D a nationally known and respected trauma surgeon for Mercy Hospital in San Diego. Relapse rates are in the 90 percent range.

Marijuana, now legal in Washington, Colorado and Oregon, is a "physiologically addicting drug...the perception that it's not dangerous is widespread. Even most kids will agree that marijuana is a so-called "gateway drug" because their tolerance increases, leading them to move on to other drugs. Because they are using an illicit drug, they are often exposed to harder drugs and to drug dealers."[6] Even if there is no escalation in drug of choice, or it is legally purchased and used, marijuana itself is twice as strong as it was twenty years ago. Mix it with alcohol or another drug and the risks skyrocket.

Another killer drug is alcohol. The possibility of alcohol poisoning, deaths from choking on vomit, or other alcohol-related death is very real. *"One quarter of all emergency room admissions, one-third of all suicides, and more than half of all homicides and incidents of domestic violence are alcohol related. Between forty-eight and sixty-four percent of people who die in fires have blood alcohol levels indicating intoxication."[7]* "Between 80-90 percent of people treated for alcoholism relapse, even after years of abstinence."[8]

Legalizing marijuana doesn't make it less lethal, just more tolerated by a society that conversely seems surprised when kids fall between the cracks or commit atrocities like murdering their parents. Washington State in their first year of legalized marijuana had about 25-33 percent increase in drivers who had active marijuana in their system when arrested. However, because there are no statistics on the increase or decrease of users because of the law, and there are problems getting samples from drivers arrested for DUIs to the lab and tested in a timely manner, it's really premature to make any assumptions.

Other drugs, including cocaine and prescription medications, have a varying degree of success for long-term recovery depending on the person, treatment program, and the drug itself. Addicts and alcoholics need professional help and a strong support system such as Alcoholics Anonymous (AA), to get them through detox and beyond. There is no vaccine to prevent addiction and no antibiotic to cure it.

I can't control it

You can't stop an addict from using. Not by loving them, threatening them, or appealing to their emotions or common sense. Emotionally your loved one is stuck near the age level when they started. See them for who they are today, not who they were, or who they might have become if they never used. Addicts lie, steal, sell their kids' stuff, or do whatever they have to do to get their next fix. They make totally outrageous promises—or more dangerous—offer plausible excuses to try to guilt you into feeling sorry for them, giving them money, and cleaning up their messes. Their mood swings confuse and scare their children who never know if they are going to get yelled at, be totally ignored, parented reasonably, or treated as their parent's best friend.

"Alcoholism is a disease of 'not yets'", said Libby, a divorced Oregon mom of five middle and high school age kids. "I learned that from Al-Anon, a twelve step program for the relatives and friends of alcoholics. *I also learned that my ex-husband, Joe, is not getting better. His desire will get worse, and he will get worse, because he does not want to quit.* He's a functioning alcoholic, with a good job, who I trust to be with the kids when he operates in my boundaries—what I'm willing to live with for the sake of the kids." For Libby this means absolutely no contact when he is drinking. She encourages scouting because, "There is zero tolerance for alcohol and it's a way for him to bond with the boys."

You cannot reach an addict until they want to be reached. Even if they are willing to change, they not you, have to do the work of getting clean and staying sober. What you can control is *your* thoughts, *your* attitude, and *your* actions. Counseling helps even if the alcoholic won't go. Mental health professionals are trained to see things we miss. They will provide *you* with insights into yours, the children's and the addict's feelings and behaviors based on what is shared, and what they observe. Every time I went with Chad when he was a toddler, and again in elementary and then high school, I learned new parenting, communication, and coping skills.

Counselors will not break confidences, so they are a safe person to talk with, except for a few well-defined areas. They must, by law, report any physical or sexual abuse and suspected neglect of minors. *Once Child Protective Services is involved, your parenting skills and ability to keep your children, or grandchildren, safe will be scrutinized along with those of your partner or adult child. The decision to stay with, or leave, your spouse, or allow grandkids' parent(s) to live with you, remains yours; however, the children's fate is, at least temporarily, out of your hands.* Please do not wait for something horrific to happen to ask for help or take action. Brandy once told me, "As a recovering alcoholic, I know you have to want to stop; if you want it bad enough you'll do it. It's that simple, but not to the active user because they don't really have a conscience—the drugs and alcohol take over."

I can take care of myself

You are a fighter. You will be a survivor. You can do whatever you have to do by facing life one day, and one step, at a time. It takes love and intense courage to say, "I won't watch you self destruct. I won't let you continue destroying your kids," and then walk away, or enforce rigid boundaries for when, where, and how they can be involved in your future.

Addicts may be passive aggressive, or try to avoid you altogether. They may respond angrily trying to sabotage, or control, conversations they don't want to have. Your job is to focus only on behavior that impacts you and the kids. Let the rest go. Do not let the alcoholic or druggie divert the attention away from themself by getting sidetracked into arguments over who said what, or why it's someone else's fault. If they become abusive, terminate the conversation and ask them to leave, or you leave. Call the police if you feel threatened. *Anything that would be a crime if a stranger did it, including stealing credit cards, selling illegal substances, threatening you, or forging a check should result in an immediate call to the police.* Even if the police don't take action, a paper trail is being established that could help you later if you sue for custody.

Don't post on social media, or allow the kids to post, any information about future vacations, trips you are on, or personal information. Sadly, we hear more and more about break-ins, family murders, and suicides—don't take chances. Restraining orders are marginally effective, but try. Vary daily routines. Ask others around you to keep watch. Protect yourself and your family by changing locks and adding alarm systems; use them always. Do not take threats lightly.

Recognize there are things you do out of love and concern for the alcoholic, or their kids, that are enabling the user's habit. Make a list and take action. Stop making wake up calls; don't cover for them with anyone, including their boss, the police, daycare, or their son or daughter. No more rides to work, emergency gas money, or groceries. Don't debate; rather tell them that you know they will figure it out. *Do* offer to pick up and take care of their children until they get sober. For safety's sake evaluate if you want to take legal action to get custody/guardianship and if you want to tell them you are doing it. If they do not let you take the kids you may need to involve children services or see an attorney to force the issue.

"Now I think what was that about? Why did I put up with it?" says native New Mexico mother, Adriana, who was married to Wes, an alcoholic, for twenty years. At the time we spoke they had two boys, one in high school and one in college. "We agreed to separate on our 20th anniversary and signed the papers on our 22nd. It was a great day when we got married, a peaceful day when we decided to divorce, and a melancholy day when it ended." In between the 'I do' and 'I'm done' were years of Wes falling flat on his face, passed out, while Adriana put Christmas toys together and covered for him with clients. She cried when her boys were humiliated at their ball games because Wes was stumbling down drunk at eleven o'clock in the morning. She was there when his parents visited. They heard his slurred speech and watched him drooling at the dinner table. They tried to pass it off as the flu until she told them, "Wes is an alcoholic. He needs help." And then she watched their tears.

Divorce, legal separation, or emancipation doesn't mean you stop loving, or praying for the alcoholic, or even from maintaining some type of controlled contact. These actions do protect you legally from future bills or legal liabilities; however, if you are married, both of you are responsible for existing debt. Pay off all bills if possible and sell, or give up, assets that you cannot afford to finance and maintain yourself. Ex's are often 'no pay' or 'slow pay' when it comes to support because no one is monitoring their drinking, spending, working, or bill paying.

Divorce presents its own challenges. Anticipate problems and have support systems in place. "When we were getting divorced, Ryan and I sat down and split costs and decided on joint custody with me having physical custody because he was using," explained Brandy. She started drinking again after ten years, in part she says, because her three daughters blamed her when their dad blew off visitations. "Looking back, I should have gotten complete custody and then I probably wouldn't have picked up the first drink." Whether you are a spouse, birth partner, or grandparent it is important to talk to an attorney at least once, to determine what rights and responsibilities you and the kids have, and how to secure them legally.

Your attitude drives everything you do and how you feel so go to counseling, join a support group, eat right, exercise, get your sleep, and have a network of friends and people you can talk to about your problems. As much as it hurts, you were probably part of the environment where the trouble began. Ouch. Al-Anon, and similar support organizations, can help you understand why separation and a new environment is as critical for continuing, or recovering, users as having your own space is vital for you and the kids.

Because you are raising children of drug users and drinkers you will never be entirely free of hurtful memories, and churning emotions; the circumstances won't let you. The intensity of your feelings may ebb and flow but you will always feel some anger, regret, frustration, relief, or sadness. Daily onslaughts happen for a while, and eventually lessen to sporadic. Events that pull you backwards are often unexpected, such as when your granddaughter angrily struggles to create a family tree, or tells you she witnessed her dad chocking his addicted girlfriend in their apartment. Other times it's a well-meaning relative asking, "Do you ever hear from Jeremy?" Sometimes, it's a news flash showing birth dad arrested for DUI, birth mom popping up on Facebook, or a teen needing a bone marrow transplant and you aren't a match. Even as an adult, if the grandkids you raise decide to reconnect and spend a holiday with their bio parent, or start calling them "my father" or "my mother" there will be unexpected twinges if they also call you mom or dad. Just when you think you are making progress, you get sucked under again and have to not only resurface, but also struggle to make it back to shore. *But you can do it.*

One of the best news articles I've read about moms of addicted children was entitled, *Being an addict's mom: "It's just a very, very sad place"*. One of the best commentaries within the story, "Viewing addiction as a disease was instrumental, many mothers say, in helping understand they didn't cause their child's addiction and couldn't fix it either…Sadly, the stigma of having a child with addiction is all too real and incredibly painful. Announce to your community your child has a disease like cancer and people will jump to help, said mothers I interviewed. Not so when you tell them your child is an addict. "There are no little girls selling cookies for addiction. Nobody has bumper stickers on the car," said [Barbara] Theodosiou."[9] There are support groups, but the public at large, still tends to wonder what you, the parent, did wrong and people hesitate to talk to you about your pain.

"You've heard this phrase over and over: *"Forgive and forget." There's only one problem with it: You can't do it. It's impossible! Because when you're trying to forget, you are actually focusing on the very thing you want to forget."*[10]

You aren't going to forget but eventually whatever is consuming your life now will fade into a manageable memory that you can tuck away and only review when, and if, you choose. It will fade faster if you talk about it with someone you trust, but don't repeat it over and over and over randomly to strangers or anyone who gossips. You need confidants who take the time to really understand and validate your feelings. People who don't judge, and help you see how far you've come rather than how far you have to go.

Don't ever try to force yourself to forget something because you will only suppress the pain. Eventually, the pain will come up and you will be miserable. I tried it for many years and finally realized that I had to face it head on. You need to come to terms with what is happening, and accept that it will change you for the better. Forgetting doesn't help, forgiving does.

"Forgiveness is not resuming a relationship without change. In fact, forgiveness and resuming a relationship are two different things...saying, "I'm sorry," is not enough... Restoring a relationship requires rebuilding trust. That, friends, takes a long, long time."[11]

If you choose not to resume a relationship with the alcoholic or addict—ever—it's okay. There is no right or wrong decision even though we push for zero contact between kids and parents. Every family, every set of circumstances, is different which is why we include examples of families with no contact, some contact, and daily contact throughout the book. Just know that you have earned the right to make the decision for yourself, and for the children you are now parenting. When these kids grow up they can, and will, make their own choices. The addict has lost their voice in the matter unless the courts keep them legally connected through shared custody, or visitations, and eventually this too will go away when minors become adults.

We owe our children—
the most vulnerable citizens in any society
a life free from violence and fear.

Nelson Mandela

2
Helping Kids Beat the Odds

Last chapter we talked about the four "C's"; you didn't cause anyone else's addiction and can't cure or control it, but *you can take care of yourself.* *Kids*, not only, didn't cause, and can't cure or control their parent's addiction, *but they cannot take care of themselves.* They did not ask to be born with Fetal Alcohol Syndrome or other genetic imperfections; all they wanted as infants was to be fed, sheltered, and loved. The longer children are neglected or physically, mentally, or emotionally abused by their birth parent(s) the more baggage they carry forward.

Sobering facts

Sons and daughters of addicts have more problems growing up, and in adulthood, than peers with non-using parents according to numerous studies. The family unit—whether parents are rich or poor, gay, single, young or old—and if the kids are only, oldest, disabled, or adopted may impact results, but the only commonality we are focused on is the impact of parental addiction. So while fatherless homes, for example, are receiving a lot of attention—and the issue needs desperately to addressed—the statistics for the sons and daughters and grand-kids you are raising are staggeringly against them. The good news is one person can make all the difference, and you are that person. You are their game changer.

- ✓ Today over 8.3 million children (11.9 per cent of children in the United States) live with a parent that either is dependent on, or abuses, drugs or alcohol resulting in "child abuse and neglect, injuries and deaths related to motor vehicle accidents, and increased odds that the children will become substance dependent or abusers themselves."[12]

- ✓ Forty one percent of children of alcoholics will develop serious coping problems by age eighteen.[13]

- ✓ *Every day in America* four children are killed by abuse or neglect while 1,837 kids are confirmed as abused or neglected.[14]

- ✓ *Foster Kids* are twice as likely as war veterans to develop post-traumatic stress disorder, and one out of every three boys will end up in jail before age nineteen, while girls in the system are twice as likely as their peers to get pregnant.[15]

- ✓ "Seventy five percent of all adolescent patients in chemical abuse centers come from fatherless homes.[16]

Children need to experience normal, to recognize what is not normal

"What happens is that the kids learn to imitate behaviors that they see as normal, and as a result, end up making the same mistakes their parents did. You would think that someone who was abused as a child would know how much it hurts and do everything they could to not do that to someone else. But instead, when they get angry as an adult they react the only way they know how, in the way that has become natural to them. With neglect, sexual abuse, substance abuse, gang membership, with all of the ugly things that exist in the world, kids tend to go back to what they know," wrote NFL football player, Michael Oher, in his book *I Beat the Odds: From Homelessness to The Blind Side and Beyond.*

One-on-one time talking about everyday things and values, as well as having fun with children, is essential. Why? Because as they relax and learn to trust you they will tell you things that let you know what they are thinking, and some of their beliefs may shock you. They may not realize that not all parents leave young elementary children to wait in a park everyday before school instead of hiring a babysitter, or that it is not okay to have sex with a boy so he will buy you clothes or drive you around. They may also be carrying burdens you know nothing about.

"If your partner is drinking and not changing early on, regardless of how much you love them, get out," says Adriana the New Mexico mother we talked about last chapter. In tears, she told me her younger son, Caleb, once said, "I wish I had a normal dad like Jason (a neighboring father) to play catch and do stuff with me." On his own, after the separation, Caleb told his dad that he would not visit him unless he had been sober for at least ten consecutive days. His older brother, Kyle, once called 911 when Adriana was out-of-town on business, thinking his dad was dying. He stood there as police and paramedics came and left saying, "No he is just drunk." Then Kyle had to figure out what to do next.

"I worried constantly because I didn't want the kids to find their father dead," Adriana recalls remorsefully. She told her sons over and over, what her therapist told her, "Your dad has a disease and needs professional help. He cannot do it by himself...its way bigger than him." She's right. The caveat is that their children need professional help also, but older youth will often fight it, and lack of money sometimes prevents it. If you are facing either of these issues Chapter Nine on counseling can give you helpful insights and resource suggestions.

Brandy choose parenting over putting Chad up for adoption when he was born, but then spent all her time looking for someone to love and take care of her--instead of learning to be independent and taking care of him. She neglected Chad long before she, and later Donald, abused him. Children who are not physically cuddled, or do not get fed or changed when they cry, will not develop empathy or boundaries. "...A growing body of scientific knowledge demonstrates that maltreatment during the nine months of fetal growth and the first twenty-four months after birth often leads to violent older children and adults."[17]

> **"It's better to build boys than mend men."**
> *S. Truett Cathy, founder Chick-fil-A*

When Chad was four, Dr. Christine Portland Ph.D. (his counselor) told me that kids with his type of history can end up as serial killers *unless they have at least one adult in their life who loves them unconditionally and who they learn to trust.* I spent the last twenty plus years making sure I was that person. I read voraciously, attended classes, took him to counseling, and always made sure that Chad knew, no matter what, that I loved him. We fought tooth and nail as you'll discover later in the book, but never, ever, did I give up on him. "You don't have to like me, but you have to show me respect." became my mantra. "Father help," my prayer.

And that's what it comes down to with love. Never give up. No matter what a child says to you, as a parent or caretaker, it's only words. I yelled at my mom until the

29

day I left for college, and now I could never say anything to hurt her. Sometimes love hurts but eventually, with work, it will become the greatest gift you receive and give in all of your life.

Chronic stress and other trauma-induced problems manifest differently depending on children's ages, personalities, and lifestyles. Even at three years old, Chad knew things weren't right with Donald and told people in the only ways he could. His body language went from normal to rigid, and his tone became hostile. His words were garbled messages for help, "Call my dad and tell him, "Chad doesn't want a new mommy, he wants his same mommy." I don't want to live with my dad. I love him. God says love everyone. He's a bad dad."

As a son, I feel like fathers have overall a huge impact, and that seeing them be an alcoholic is extremely hurtful. From my youngest days I have had a lasting impression of what alcohol does to families. Donald was an alcoholic: he drank, what seemed like, every night. I remember mornings of not being able to wake him up, and thinking that he had died; it scared me to death and mom says I talked about it a lot. Alcoholism amongst fathers is a very big issue, but the damage from mothers who over drink is just as severe. I remember that I was worried about becoming an alcoholic like my birth father and mother, and still today my wife is always helping me make sure that I don't. I couldn't, and can't, outrun the alcoholism issue.

Building trust

Even when you understand why children are acting out, it can still be difficult to remain calm and patient because it often takes years to peal back all of the layers of damage. Their anger often masks their fear or pain. Lying helped them survive. It they were sexually, or physically, abused any sudden movement or physical touch may set off memories and reactions that they can't block. For years Chad would not let me out of his sight, and when he did start watching TV in an adjacent room he'd huddle into one corner of the couch. He'd call out my name frequently to make sure I was still there, and if there were any sudden movements or loud noises he'd jump. Symptoms lessened over the years but didn't go away entirely until he was in his late teens.

Empoweringparents.com is a great resource offering practical parenting tips for handling difficult behaviors. James Lehman, one of the site founders, said before his passing that children, "watch us for a living." The very act of covering for your partner or adult child, regardless of your intentions, weakens your trust-worthiness with their kids. *You cannot move forward until this trust erosion is repaired.* Never make a promise you can't keep. Don't lie, and don't cover for anyone. Better to say things like, "We'll talk about it when you are older", or "it is never okay to sell drugs and what you dad did was wrong regardless of how he tries to shift the blame" or "that's between your mother and myself."

My wife and I have an agreement that no one else will ever see us get upset at one another, but we do have healthy disagreements that people sometimes see and respect our resolutions. *Some conflicts should be private.* This is especially true when there is a child that has an addict as parent. They are already seeing things that they shouldn't, and if they then see that the sober parent is belligerent, it can scar them even more. It is important to show kids conflict resolution, but this should teach them that it does not involve yelling, arguing, and irrational behavior.

I've found in talking with kids being raised by alcoholics and addicts, and reading their social posts, *almost everyone in their life—adults as well as their friends—have skewed values and low expectations for themselves and others.* It's a long road back to ground zero for these children, but with your help they can get there.

Develop an action plan

Chemical dependency is complex. When asked, "At what point is a person beyond rational decision making?" Dr. Sise answered, "The very first time they use methamphetamine, and within one hour of using it. This why we need to get to low-intensity users quickly before methamphetamine permanently affects the brain."[18]

In 1997 congress realized kids from drug families were staying in foster care for years, or revolving in and out and back in again. Parents were not getting better after a series of classes or a session in a rehab center. So, the Adoption and Safe Families Act (ASFA) was passed requiring a permanent place-ment decision for any minor in government custody for fifteen, or more, months out of the past twenty-two. *I'm for an even shorter time frame if the user relapses once, or isn't trying after a few months of counseling or rehab.*

Go for the most permanent custodial arrangement possible, which is adoption. It cannot be reversed by the birth parent down the road if they hit a prolonged patch of stability that looks to last into their children's adulthood—although we don't recommend it unless you are terminally ill or some other life-changing event occurs. In 2000 the United States Supreme Court essentially ruled in Troxel Vs. Granville that biological parents have a constitutional right expressed in a presumption that they act in the best interest of their children. This stan-dard does not serve children of addicts. If even short-term users' brains are altered, then their ability to get, and keep, rea-sonably paying jobs and make good parenting choices is jeopardized. Judges can, and often do, take children away from relatives who have raised them for years, or give the birth parent visitation rights in the misguided assumption that mom or dad will not relapse, and will always put their children's needs ahead of their own.

Soul searching

"My husband was *addicted to alcohol* and I *was addicted to the alcoholic.*"[19] Profound. Honest. Scary. Get counseling for yourself if you need it. Don't stay married to an alcoholic or addict to keep your home, bank account, or social life intact. Be aware, as Libby's counselor cautioned her, of remarrying someone with the same personality traits, addictions, or relationship expectations as your former partner because it feels familiar, or you are lonely.

Again, you didn't cause your loved one to drink or use drugs, and you can't cure, or control them. However, *anything you do that enables them to further hurt their children is now on you. Not making a decision is it's own decision.*

Your life does not get better by chance, it gets better by change.

Jim Rohn, Author & Speaker

3
Handling the Legal Stuff—Part One: Adoption, Guardianship, Custody & Related Matters

Legally speaking

Trying to cure a heart attack, or cancer, without seeking medical help is like trying to handle legal issues without talking to an attorney. *None of us knows what we don't know, and that's the problem. When parental rights, physical/legal custody and guardianship, or adoption are involved the consequences of ignorance, or error, are too great to gamble.* No one wants to take away a parent's rights, but sometimes it's necessary. Chad and I aren't legally trained or licensed. Again, we are sharing information, experiences, and resources that we have gleaned from professionals, other families, and our own journey.

Legal matters involving addicts/alcoholics and their children can be extremely complex and often *criminal* (DUIs or theft), *civil* (companies suing you for credit card debt) and *family court* (custody or divorce) proceedings are happening in different courts in the same general time frame. Because laws vary from state to state, and family court judges have individual differences, a local lawyer is immensely important.

The only attorney representing you is the one you retain

A court appointed attorney represents their designated client— usually the birthparent or the child—not you. Since many addicts have a low paying, or no job, they often get free representation. Children who are wards of the court also have their own attorney provided by the state. Once a judge deems that a minor can have a say in who has guardianship and custody over them, and if they do not want to be with you, their lawyer regardless of their opinion, is obligated to argue for their wishes.

Every agency has in-house legal counsel whose job it is to protect the government and its employees from lawsuits. Caseworkers may say, or imply, that they are going to make certain recommendations regarding child placement and/or parental rights. However, things can change. Their supervisor may disagree with their decision. Your case may be re-assigned to another caseworker who wants to try to put the family back together, or place the children with someone else. There may be a change in administrative policy, management, or law. *Never rely on the state to protect your interests.*

You need your own attorney, or you need to petition the court for legal standing as an intervener, if you want to participate in court procedures unless you are the other bio parent. This gives you access to pre-trial reports, caseworker and CASA recommendations, and other vital information. Legal standing assures you a voice if the state has, or obtains, legal guardianship and decides to place the child with another relative, in a non-relative foster home, or supervised care facility.

Sadly, the availability of low, or no cost, legal services are declining while costs are increasing.[20]

Support groups are excellent places to ask about local legal resources and get recommendations from others in your situation. You'll want a lawyer experienced in the areas where you need help, and one who has a record of successes. Ask up front about fees and other expenses. If you can't afford a lawyer start calling organizations such as AARP, the American Bar Association Center on Children and the Law, your state bar association, U.S. Department of Health and Human Services Administration for Children and Families Child Welfare Information Gateway, Children's Defense Fund, state Foster Parents Association, and law schools to see if they can recommend any attorneys who will take your case on a sliding scale, or work for free. Always write down questions you want to ask, and have personal information well organized and with you, so you make every minute count when you do talk to an attorney or referral resource.

Parental rights, kid rights, your rights

If you decide to represent yourself, seriously consider having an attorney advise you on how to proceed and then, at the end, review the legal rulings and paperwork. Often people do some things themselves and have a lawyer handle other pieces. I held a sobbing California grandmother who never filed the final adoption papers, and subsequently ended up losing all rights to even visit the granddaughter she had raised for eight years. Her son, the father, was newly sober, newly married, and lived out-of- state. Her granddaughter did not want to go live with him, but the judge said her hands were tied. This grandma's story about legal misadventures is not unique. Relatives have shared other heartbreaking experiences, including having the children they raised decide in their teens to live with a using, or newly recovering, addict/ alcoholic. For birth parents this may result in not only losing custody, but also in having to pay future child support.

Adoption is almost always my first recommendation. If the addict's parental rights aren't terminated then the door is left open for them to file for returned custody, joint custody, and/or guardianship of their children. Adoption shuts that door. Kids can stop worrying. You can stop worrying. If something happens to you, then your spouse (if they also adopt them) or a designated guardian, not the birthparents, will have custody.

I wasn't worried when I was little because I didn't know legal stuff or think about having to live with my birth parents again. I never knew when legal things were happening; I was just really happy when dad adopted me that we were going to be a family and all have the same last name.

Legal guardianships and/or custody that cannot be challenged at a later time by a biological parent are called specialized durable guardianship in Oregon, but terms vary by state. Durable guardianships are typically the exception; most guardianship can be modified, or dismissed, if a judge is convinced the parent is capable of meeting minimal parenting standards. Can't stress it enough--if you have the opportunity to permanently assume control—take it. No matter how well an addict eventually does, or does not do, their kids deserve one home from here on out. You can always allow contact with the bio parent if you choose to, but the decision should be yours, not the courts.

Although we mentioned it earlier, it's important to repeat that the 2000 ruling on Troxel v. Granville in essence *forces family judges to look at possibilities for the birth parent's future, not the underwhelming odds against sustained recovery.* It totally ignores the fact that children of addicts often have trauma-induced wounds (for many its Post Traumatic Stress Syndrome) and that minimally functioning parents cannot provide the stable, patient, and kid-focused home environment they need to cope and heal.

Try to help the addict see that voluntarily relinquishing parental rights is best for them and their kids. Explain that they can contact their son or daughter after high school; you can't prevent it anyway once the children reach legal age, which is often during their senior year. If they say, "no", then petition the court to terminate parental rights. All states have provisions for involuntary termination of rights and most consider severe or chronic abuse/neglect, abandonment, and "long-term alcohol-or drug-induced incapacity of the parent(s)," to be sufficient grounds for doing so.[21]

Strictly adhere to all legalities including making a substantial effort to locate missing biological parents, using proper forms, posting legal notification of pending court procedures, and filing judgments. This reduces the risk of parents later having a decision overturned because of procedural or processing errors.

A lawyer may tell you that your chance of getting legal custody, changing visitation orders, or adoption is slim based on law and precedents. As cold as it sounds, don't throw away your money; money that often comes from retirement funds or loans as everything else, it seems, goes for day-to-day expenses. On the other hand, I won a very convoluted and uphill battle.

Documentation is another just way of saying keep notes

Jot things down so you don't forget. It can be done with a notebook, scraps of paper stuffed into an envelope, on your iPad, or any method that works for you. Keep copies of emails and written comments from teachers, youth leaders, coaches, and counselors. Include the date, time, who was present, what happened, and what was said. Also, note the impact on the child, for example:

July 14, 3003. Dad didn't show, or call, for third weekly scheduled visit in a row. No questions or comments from Heather.

July 28, 3003 Ms. Murphy, Austin's teacher, reported he was acting out in class again—see attached email stating pattern of misbehavior following visits.

September 12, 3003: Cynthia missed school because of a migraine headache that started last night about 15 minutes after her mother called. Cynthia volunteered that her mom has been asking her for money and "gets angry when I tell her I don't have any".

Before important meetings and hearings prepare a one-page paper (any longer and it won't get read) that highlights key points that you want addressed or feel are helpful to your case. Use lots of white space, bullets, and limit it to three sections as shown below.

Re: Joan Callander Dingle seeking adoption of grandson, Jed Smith

Contact: **Attorney Jess Brown;** 555.888.9999, Brown & Associates P.C., Jbrown3003@gmail.com.

Date: Use day of hearing or meeting.

Requested action:
- Retain temporary custody.
- Set hearing date for revoking parental rights for within 30 days.

- Obtain a restraining order against Harold, the biological father.

Significant factors:
- Mother has not had any contact in 3 years; father failed to complete court ordered parenting or anger management classes.
- Father has threatened to abduct Jed and take him to another country.
- Jed's counselor has recommended no further contact with either parent. He needs meds to get to sleep and wakes up with blood-curdling screams 2-3 times nightly.

Pertinent background:
- Jed is severely autistic. Bio parents physically abused Jed at different ages. His mother did prison time for her abuse, and his dad lost custody and visitation rights.
- Father is out on bail pending charges of armed robbery. He was arrested last weekend for possession of a controlled substance and a stolen gun.
- There have been three caseworkers, four prosecuting attorneys, and two state-appointed attorneys for Jed since (name of state) assumed custody four years ago.

Ask your attorney if it would be appropriate to give copies to the other attorneys and pertinent players. Most social workers and government attorneys are busy, and understaffed. They frequently do not have time to familiarize themselves thoroughly with each case, and *may be* influenced, at least subconsciously, by your efforts.

Prepping for, and presenting in court

If testifying, your lawyer should coach you about questions to expect, and how to frame your answers. Be clear and concise. *State facts, not opinions.* For example, "Penny smelled of alcohol, and she fell on the first stair up to our apartment while carrying the baby","" rather than, "Penney was drunk again when she brought the kids home." *Paint emotional word pictures,* "Liam was clutching my leg while screaming, "I don't want to go with my dad. I hate him." *Witnesses for your side—including counselors and physicians—need to do the same.* Ask them to use every day language, and limit clinical terms. You want the judge to understand both the damage done by the addict, and future risks the parent poses to their children.

If there are multiple lawsuits and/or criminal charges pending, the criminal cases are typically resolved before custody issues are finalized. Anything you say in one court can be used in the others, so if you misspeak—or someone else misquotes you--correct the record even if it seems trivial, "I want to make sure that I didn't mislead anyone, what I meant to say was," or "for the record, I did not say that Jack's dad gave him meth. I stated that the school counselor called me to report the staff, in a random locker check, found meth in Jack's locker after his dad dropped him off at the high school last month."

If you are asked two questions at the same time, clearly separate the issues, and answer each individually. For example, "The answer to the first part of your question is, "Yes, I did see George hit Mike on multiple occasions", as to the second part, "No I did not physically try to stop George on March 3rd as he threatened to hurt Mike and I with his knife." Be respectful, not argumentative or defensive. Don't make generalized negative statements about social workers, or the court system. Not all social workers are inept, or all judges biased. Dress nicely, not provocatively or too informal, but not looking all stiff and too busy to parent either. Be cautious about anything you say within several blocks of a courthouse, and definitely within its courtrooms, hallways, and bathrooms.

Attend all hearings, even if you expect a postponement, because judges are not always predictable. With Chad's birth dad, the judge called him when he didn't show up after asking for postponements at two previous court appearances. Deciding that Donald could have made the hearing by taking a bus or calling a friend, the judge ruled on Chad's future placement without him present.

Kids, in my opinion, don't belong in court. They don't need to hear all the ugly details, and if they are young they don't even need to know you are heading to court because they won't understand, or they will worry. In a pre-custody hearing Chad's dad, Donald, said, "If it takes a beating with a two-by-four to get the child's attention, that's what you use." Of course I did not tell Chad, but I did make sure that every caseworker, district attorney, and court appointed attorney for him heard about it at the start of each subsequent meeting and/or court date. Minors can testify but because of the very difficult position it puts them in think carefully before initiating it. It is possible that the courtroom can be cleared if both sides and the judge agree, or testimony can be in chambers with or without parents/lawyers—but there will be a court reporter or videotaping. Discuss this with your legal advisor and the child's therapist or doctor.

I don't think minors should testify in court unless they are the only one(s) who can persuade the judge because they are coming from a hard place already, and will not make rational decisions like an adult usually would. At that point in life, they may be afraid to hurt somebody's feelings whether it's a parent, grandparent or even a best friend of theirs who thinks they should live with the addict or alcoholic.

Testifying against your adult child or partner may be the most gut-wrenching thing you ever have to do

I remember vividly how the cold marble tiles echoed as I walked down the hall and pulled open the heavy wooden door

42

to the courtroom where I would fight Brandy for guardianship, and custody, of Chad (adoption came later). She didn't understand that even if he was only four his anger was so out-of-control that he broke furniture by shaking it. He once kicked my then boyfriend, and now husband Bob, when he was lying propped up on his elbow on the floor so hard that it caused his arm to collapse. She wanted to get pregnant and told the judge her 'sex life' was her own business not understanding that the unborn child (and Chad who would have been taken from her if anything happened) would be in danger.

I had on a gray and white business dress while she wore something better suited for a garden wedding. Brandy told the judge that she'd try to get Chad to counseling but it was a long way to drive. I wanted to shake her because her answer should have been, "I'd walk on coals to get my son the help he needs." When the judge ruled in my favor, her in-laws formed a protective circle around her while I slowly walked alone to my car. I was, as I was frequently in those days, physically and emotionally drained. If I had lost, Chad lost. When I won, I lost.

All you can do is walk it through. No grandparent has kids so they can later parent grandkids; no couple gets married to go through a divorce. It is the presence of love that causes pain—not the lack of it.

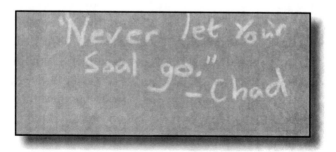

From a Mother's Day book of poems Chad, age 9.

There is a ripple effect from every action in life—good or bad. Brandy *had six children with four different dads.* One son she allowed to be adopted through an agency—helping to select the family; he was a dad before the age of twenty. Another of her sons died when her placenta separated from her uterus while she was in jail—his remains were given to her in a lunch box. Chad's oldest half-sister, raised by Brandy and Ryan together and then separately after their divorce, started having sex at age twelve. Another sister has such low self-esteem that her posts on Facebook break your heart. The youngest told her school counselor that she was raped. Brandy's choices caused, and continue to cause, a lot of pain. *However your choices turn out, you'll never know what other bad things might have happened if you do nothing.*

Common legal terms

CASA: A court appointed special advocate (CASA) is a trained volunteer who is a neutral person in juvenile court proceedings. They gather information and submit their assessment of current placements, and make recommendations for future placement, of children to the judge. Their recommendations are not binding.

Childcare subsidy: Financial aid, administered through the state, for day care.

Child support: Generally, it is the duty of the non-custodial biological parent to pay a court ordered amount of money for care of their child to the custodial parent unless parental rights are terminated. It is not as cut and dry with third parties, and sometimes the seeking of support can so anger a biological parent that they will thwart your efforts for custody. Whether you pay or receive support arrange for it to be handled through the court so that there is a paper trail. This protects all parties.

Civil court: The court system where lawsuits are filed by individuals, groups or corporations alleging wrongdoing, based on law. Juries render verdicts, and damages are monetary.

Criminal court: The court where government charges individuals or legal entities with breaking the law, and juries decide the outcome. Defendants found guilty of crimes including DUIs, theft, murder, etc. are typically sentenced to jail time, probation, community service, and/or fines.

Custody: *Legal custodians* have the right to make decisions, such as medical care needs, for a child or person of diminished capacity. *Physical custodians have the person living with them.*

Family court: In this court there is no jury; judge's decision is 'final'; however, can be appealed. Cases typically involve divorce, child support, custody, guardianship, and paternity.

Guardian: A court appointed person who has the right to decide physical, medical, or educational needs for another person. Sometimes the court will appoint a conservator to manage a child's or disabled person's financial affairs.

Intervener: A person with a vested interest, who is permitted to participate in an existing court case, but is not the defendant or the initiator of the case.

Juvenile court: Special court dealing with crimes by minors, or against children by other family members.

Mandated reporter: Persons stipulated by law who must report any suspected child abuse to authorities including teachers, counselors, doctors, social workers and nurses.

Mediator: A person trained to help work out agreements to resolve issues before going to court, or in lieu of, a court hearing. By law, most mediation communications are confidential and cannot be used in court proceedings unless the mediation leads to a written agreement.

Petition: The legal papers filed to initiate a case.

Power of Attorney: A document that gives another person legal authority to act on another's behalf in all, or specifically stated, matters. It must be notarized. It is important to check with an attorney or a state government employee to determine the various types of power of attorney documents that can be used, the proper terms, the duration of time that they remain valid if unrevoked, and their strengths and pitfalls.

Protective custody: Temporary removal of a person from their home for their protection—typically only used in short-term emergency situations.

Psychological parent: A person who has spent a substantial amount of time with a minor, and one with whom the minor has bonded--as they would bond with a parent. Some states recognize two classifications: A psychological parent who has served in the custodial role, and a person with an "ongoing personal relationship" for those who have had a significant, but non-custodial, role.

Trust: Funds or property set aside for care of, or use by, an individual. A trustee handles funds according to creator's instructions.

Don't give up. Grow stronger.

Frequently asked questions with legal implications

There are numerous difficulties that we all face in life, having an addict in the family just piles on complexities. Some issues involving financial assistance, estate planning, visitations, medical or educational disabilities are talked about in the next chapters or throughout the book. The following are not intended to be all-inclusive in subject matter, or response.

46

Can I enroll my grandkids, a foster child, or other minor who lives with me in school if I do not have a court order or legal custody papers?

Generally yes; however, you may need proof of their residing with you such as post-marked letters addressed to the child at your address or copies of bills for their food or medical care. In order to have access to their records, or prevent their parents from accessing their records, you will need to meet certain legal requirements.

I have a job (or pension) but it's not enough. Can I receive financial help? What legal documents will I need?

Whether parent or grandparent, you or the child, may qualify for government programs to help with expenses including child-care subsidy. Some examples are Temporary Assistance to Needy Families (TANF), food stamps, and social security benefits if you are retired or a birth parent is deceased. Always call and ask if you qualify because some are *child only* income based, while others consider your assets and income, and others just your income. The documentation requirements vary including those for illegal immigrants.

Can I get free medical care for the children, or be reimbursed for out-of-pocket expenses?

There is no way to answer these two questions without specifics; however, there are many more resources for health coverage today than in years past. States offer insurance for children of low-income families. Some, like Michigan, require a prosecuting attorney seek court ordered child support for any child receiving public assistance (FIP or Medicaid) or if the grandparent has been appointed by the court as guardian.[22] However, if you are not willing to pay or have the birth parent ultimately held responsible, do not sign. Be completely honest when making any appointment or seeking medical care for anyone including yourself. If you have a child insured under a private policy—the terms of the policy will dictate what expenses, if any, they will reimburse if you pay up front.

My child or grandchild has some Native American blood; do I have to notify anyone special if I want to adopt?

The Indian Child Welfare Act gives federally registered tribes certain rights to be notified and involved in custody, education, and other matters. It applies when the biological parent and/or their child is a tribal member, or eligible for tribal membership. The tribal rights typically supersede state and non-Native American familial rights. Many tribes provide their tribal members with cash, college tuition, and other benefits.

Why can't I just look up legal advice or download forms from the Internet?

You can. However, the information is only as reliable as its source, its timeliness, the application to your circumstances, and adherence to the law when applying it. Use the web as a resource for gathering information, refining questions, and expanding possible contacts. Narrow down what you want an attorney's services for—including advice, review, and/or representation. All situations involving children, addicts, and law have some commonalities, and some uniqueness. What applies to your friend, or applied to Chad and I, may not work for you.

Life is what happens to us when
we are busy making plans.

John Lennon

4
Handling the Legal Stuff—Part Two: Wills, Estates, and Family Talks

Who do you want to take care of your kids, or grandkids, if something happens to you? Do you want to leave the addict or alcoholic any of your personal possessions, other assets, or money? Do you want to provide the addict or special needs child long-term financial assistance, or help with living expenses? What, if any, responsibilities are your other adult children interested in providing for their nieces and nephews and/or sibling? These are just a few questions to ask yourself, and then discuss acceptable options with potential guardians, and an experienced attorney.

Estate planning and creation of a will are critical for all adults. Inheritance is a gift, not a right, unless you die without having made a will. Then the state assigns "rights" to your relatives that may be contradictory to your wishes and are harmful for them, or hurt other family members. If you don't have a will then a judge—not to be redundant but it bears repeating--who does not know you, your family's history, or the minors in your care, will make guardianship decisions. All money, and possessions, will be distributed according to the state laws where you live.

The addict

Begin your estate planning by making choices concerning the addict. Realistically, decisions about them impact most other decisions because you are raising their kids. If you think they would be the best parenting option if you become incapacitated or die, then figure out the legalities and move on. If not, and the rest of the chapter, as well as book, assumes you do not for all the reasons we've talked about previously, then designate someone else. *If the biological parent's rights haven't been revoked, or if the state has legal guardianship, this could be problematic.* Ask your lawyer what is possible, and prudent, regarding guardianship and dividing your assets to help whomever steps up to parent, while being fair to the rest of your family.

There are many things to consider regardless if you choose to leave money or personal belongings to a user or not; we can't tell you what to do and no one else inside your family, or out, has any right to harass, try to change your mind, or judge, you. After twenty-four years, I walked away from Brandy, and I'm not enabling her in my death. I am not disowning her; I'm disinheriting her. I still love and pray for her—but I realize I can't change her. I revised my will several times over the last twenty years as I painfully, and prayerfully, considered what I thought was best for my daughter, her daughters, Chad and the rest of my wonderful, and ever-expanding, family. I wish things were different but I'm trying to hold my peace with the fact that they are not.

If you disinherit a son or daughter, say so in your will and any other 'last wishes' documents and explain why. This minimizes grounds for their claiming oversight, diminished capacity, or legal incompetency on your part. Your attorney will probably recommend (and if they don't—ask about) adding a clause to your will stating that if it is contested all legal expenses must be paid by those bringing the suit, not the estate. Things are a bit more complicated when it comes to partners, so regardless if legally separated, married and living together or apart, or in a common law relationship talk to a lawyer sooner, rather than later. If divorced make sure your 'ex' is not still a beneficiary or co-owner on any life insurance policies, deeds, financial accounts, and titles for property, RVs, boats, or cars.

It is absolutely okay to include the addict as a beneficiary. Some parents bequeath only practical items such as a used car or clothes—rather than cash. Some set up a trust, with what would have been the user's share, to go instead toward raising their children. Any monies not used can be given to your other children and/or grandchildren when they become of age--or at any designated age such as twenty-five when they'd be less likely to squander it. Other moms or dads prefer to create a 'wait and see' option requiring the user to be clean and sober for a stated period of time, generally coupled with an age requirement, for example: "Jeffrey must be free from all alcohol or drug use for five years by the time he is forty or the money set aside as his share is to be distributed among the remaining heirs equally." There is also the option of holding money aside to cover future living, or medical, expenses if they become incapacitated. However, if the addict receives financial help for housing, medical, schooling, or living expenses through government programs, such as Supplemental Security Income (SSI), welfare or Medicare, there may be limits on what assets and /or income can be in their name. Even small inheritances could disqualify them, again making legal consultation, vital.

The addict, sibs, and your money

The alcoholic's siblings may resent it, if you leave anything to their chemically abusive brother or sister. It is highly likely that you have already spent a disproportionate amount of money on the addict and his, or her, kids. Since your other children, and not the alcoholic, probably will continue being there for you now, and as circumstances change in the future, their feelings are understandable. It may be psychologically easier for them if you provide a lump sum for the user's care, or make the addict a sole beneficiary of an IRA, life insurance policy, or a special needs trust set up to make limited, direct payments to a life-care facility if you choose to do anything.

As the child of an alcoholic I would feel angry if Brandy were to get anything from my mom. She deserves nothing. My brothers and I have done so much more for mom, but even if she didn't want to give us anything, at least her brothers and sisters or a charity, would use the money wisely. Brandy hurt my mom in more ways than I can imagine, even after all she did for her. It was good when mom finally disinherited her and walked away.

Someone has to manage funds if they are not immediately dispersed. Ask yourself, "Do I want my sober sons or daughters to have to be their brother or sister's keeper?" Besides the time commitment, it could cause further resentment on both sides... one having to ask, the other having to say 'no' if requests don't meet your stipulations. A paid professional eliminates these issues and provides safety for your family if the alcoholic, or their acquaintances, have a history of violence. On the other hand, whoever takes over parenting the addict's kids (except for the addict who will probably blow any money you leave on booze or drugs) should have discretionary decision power and direct access to any funds you leave for the young ones' upbringing. The larger your estate the more complex the issues, and the more important it is to have your accountant and attorney communicate before any final decisions are made. Tax implications vary hugely from state to state and may impact how you want to structure your holdings and bequeaths.

Guardianship decisions

The best placements for children are not always the first people who come to mind. Family members may be a perfect fit, or for a myriad of reasons, not. If a son, daughter, spouse or their children, aren't on board, it won't work. Single adult family members may have a job, personality, or life style that isn't conducive to parenting. Single adults may also be exactly the right match, but consider carefully what things in their life, and your young ones' lives, are changeable and what are not.

You shouldn't choose guardians for your child based just on what you want. What it comes down to is where your child will feel wanted and safe. All you have to ask yourself is, "Where is their home away from home now, or who would be their next best forever family if you aren't here?"

When Chad was in elementary school, he and one of my nephews who were close in age did not get along. My brother and sister-in-law were willing to raise Chad, and he loved them, but it wouldn't have been good for my brother's family or for Chad. Chad was not wild about my second choice as guardians, who were close family friends, **"Because they have girls!"** A few years later, that girl thing was not so bad. A few more years and my choice changed again because Chad's best friend, and his best friend's parents, was already his second family.

Obviously, whoever you think would be a good match needs to be consulted; they may say "yes" or "no", and their rationale may confirm your decision, or send you in a different direction. Listen and stay open. If a son, daughter, or other close relative is not your first or second choice, explain to them why you are thinking of an alternative. If you don't talk now you'll never have a chance to clarify your rationale, and they'll never have a chance to challenge your assumptions, expand your thought process, or agree with you. What you think is in their best interest may pierce their heart, take a burden off their mental shoulders, or make them angry. Talk is cheap, but the results are priceless.

Special needs children

Someone you know who has children with similar life experiences, or special needs, can be a really good choice for custody and/or guardianship. Don't discount anyone because you think they are too busy, or overwhelmed with the demands of their own children. People in analogous circumstances already know the rewards, and challenges, facing them. They probably know how to work with the government, mental health, and education agencies and systems that your son or daughter needs. "Watch how the person you are considering relates to your child, or grandchild, when no one is around. *Listen to how their children talk about your child...it tells you a lot*," says Brian Rubin an Illinois attorney with a special needs son who also handles legal issues for special needs families. Some people, he continued, "say they are willing [to be a guardian] but they do not understand the demands and commitment." Protecting and providing for progeny of alcoholics or drug users is a responsibility that may continue for years if a 'special needs' child grows into a 'special needs' adult. Always appoint an alternate guardian, and review your decision every year. Life happens and the ability, and willingness, to parent changes.

Transitioning with sensitivity and logic

If you become seriously ill, or die, the first days will be painful and chaotic for everyone; it doesn't matter how well the kids and their new caregivers know each other. While grieving another loss, the young ones will have to adjust to a new home, possibly new friends, new rules, and living with a different family. The adult will be trying to manage their career, other family members' insecurities and feelings, their own grief, and

54

probably anger with the addict and/or God. So anything you can do to ease the transition by writing down vital information, as well as some critical 'heart' stuff, is a labor of love from you to them. Tell them now where the information is stored, and give them the password if it's on your computer, iPad, or smart phone.

Helpful stuff to know immediately

➤ The names and contact information for schools, teachers, carpool drivers, and kids' best friends, doctors, dentists, and counselors. Mention where to find your calendar for scheduled doctor and dental appointments, music lessons, youth/school activities, etc. If a negative situation, such as bullying, exists write about it and name names. Conversely, if there is an adult or peer who the kids are especially close to, again name names.

➤ If medications are needed then note their location, the dosage, time of day given, prescribing provider, and reason it is being taken. With some meds even brief lapses are critical, if so include instructions in case of a missed dosage. If a generic substitution is a health risk, or ineffective, say so.

➤ Include caseworkers' contact information and all government programs providing benefits, such as food stamps, Medicaid, or SSI. Jot down if it's the birth parent, yourself, or the child who is the client of record; include vital information, such as social security or case numbers that they will need to provide. If an addict, or child with special needs, is in a group home or assisted living facility give payment information, and mention where progress reports and long-term care plans are kept.

➤ Record policy numbers for medical and life insurance, your agent's name, and their phone number.

➤ Disclose favorite and hated foods, allergy information, and special circumstances. Two examples: I promised Chad he never had to eat tomatoes, as his dislike for them dated back to the four-hour beating that landed Brandy in jail and Chad in foster care. Also, I have a niece who is deadly allergic to peanuts, and if anyone even touches a plate that had something with peanuts in it and then her plate she can die without immediate medical attention. In the case of severe allergies make sure to say where EPI pens are kept, and if the child knows how to self-medicate.

➤   Describe or attach pictures of special toys, blankets, clothes, TV programs, or activities that could cause a melt down if missing. If a child is afraid of dogs, spiders, dark haired men, swimming, or other things—get it down on paper.

➤   Give critical insights such as: Always use a calm voice and never make a sudden move or Lola flashes back to the abuse from her mom's 'boyfriends', and she cowers or hides.

In addition to the short list, keep a detailed record. Include previous items and add immunization records, hobbies, bank account information, IEP (Individual Education Plan), yours and the other biological parent(s)' name, social security number, and a brief chronological sequence of events and legal rulings. Describe visitation arrangements and whether court ordered, or voluntary. Include copies of restraining orders, wills, passports, birth certificates, and adoption papers.

Create a family genealogy and attach medical information for the birth family, as well as, your family if you are a grandparent. Biological medical histories can be crucial, depending on what happens in the kids' lives.

In every person there is a need to know where you came from, it may not surface until you are older, but it happens. I always thought of my adoptive family as my only family; still as I got older, I wanted to know who I was both medically and culturally. I wanted to see what

Donald looked like now—I only have two pictures of him taken just before I went to live with him. If something had happened to mom she left enough information for me to track him down, but in the end Donald's sister contacted me and asked if I wanted to reconnect with him.

Make a life book with the "heart memory stuff" you find in baby books that might otherwise be lost, like when the child took their first steps, their favorite movies at various ages, and pictures of them and their parents. A love letter of your thoughts, feelings, and dreams for them would be treasured forever. Jessica's grandpa read her deceased grandmother's diary entry on the day Jessica was born—at their wedding reception--and there wasn't a dry eye in the house.

Kids think your old age is all about them

The generational gap can't be avoided. No matter what age your child is, and what age you are, they are always a part of a different generation. Each generation does things differently, and to a teenager, they don't care about the age variance, they just use it as an excuse. Realize that there will always be differences, accept and work through them.

"Grandma and grandpa are old and will die, and what will happen to me?" is a worry counselors often hear. With one, or both, parents missing from their lives even if you are young— the fear exists. Random terrorism and increasing street/school violence also keep anxiety, and death, in their everyday lives in ways that other generations never faced. Kids and teens won't usually tell you straight out what they are worrying over— often they don't consciously know-- so you need to initiate periodic discussions.

Age is relative. To a toddler the teen babysitter is old, and to a teen thirty is ancient. I clearly remember Chad telling me, when he was in the fifth grade, to drop him off rather than walk in with him to a church youth function. I explained that because of the large facility and low staffing at that hour, I needed to make sure an adult was there. He was adamant that I not go in. Finally he said, "**Your wrinkles embarrass me.**" Daggers to my heart. Even though he immediately said, "**I'm sorry, I didn't mean it.**" *He had meant it, and he did not need to apologize.* I was older than the pony-tailed moms of his classmates. I told him, "I can dye my hair or lose weight but I cannot erase my wrinkles." He went on to say, "**You aren't old, you're only ten years older than Ryan W's dad.**" It obviously was a big enough deal that he had not only talked to his friend, but also calculated the age difference. We talked about it again when I picked him up, and occasionally over the years. I let him know that I understood his feelings. I also made sure he knew the "where you'll live" stuff because the surface message is not the only issue. *Knowing he would not be going back to either his birth parents, or be in a foster home, was what he needed to hear.*

Kids crave reassurance. Let them know you are healthy, unless you are in poor health or terminally ill and then the conversations about guardianship and the legal work are even more essential. Talk on a level they understand, but always be honest. Tell them frequently that they are wanted, valued, and loved; make sure your actions mirror your words. I told Chad repeatedly, "I love you," but I did not tell him how much I loved being his mom. The two are different. One means, "You are lovable," the other means, "You are my son and I'm so proud; also, you have family who have your back." Chad needed, and needs to know, "Whether I am at home waiting for you to come through the door, or in heaven smiling down, I will always love you and cherish every minute of the time we have had together." I want him to be independent and happy. I want him to try things and to realize that mistakes are just opportunities to try something else. I want him to honor God, and to make faith and family his top priorities—in that order. He will always be one of the great loves of my life, and I want him to know these things deep within his head, heart, and soul.

A few added thoughts

Talking is important, but it doesn't mean a thing if you don't do the legal paperwork. It's pretty hard for your grown son or daughter to take a verbal promise to the bank, or to convince a judge that, "Mom wanted me to raise Jeremiah". If kids end up back with a birth parent, in a foster home, or with someone other than who you discussed, it's one more betrayal in their young lives. You become another adult who didn't keep their promise, another person they loved who abandoned them. *So please don't procrastinate.* Get your affairs in order, and then move on to the fun things ahead.

If you don't have an attorney, or don't know where to start looking for one, reread last chapter and add the following resources to your list. When special needs are in play for minors or the addict, contact the Special Needs Alliance, or The ARC For People with Intellectual and Developmental Disabilities for both information and referrals. Lawyers sometimes volunteer as speakers for support groups or community classes. Attending these volunteer presentations is a good way to gather information, evaluate the professional, and talk to other attendees about their experiences. It is not an arena intended for extended case specific questions, although often these professionals will talk to you *briefly* one-on-one during a break or after their presentation. If you don't have the money up front, call their office later and ask about reduced fees and/ or payment arrangements.

"I think, each time you get older, your soul gets a little closer to God. Every night it counts down until it gets to zero, and then you're dead," a very young Chad exclaimed one night after completing his prayers. Most of us don't know when we're a breath away from zero. Take care of the legal stuff now because a nanosecond after zero it's too late.

We affect the generations to come
with the decisions that we make today.

Joel Olsteen, Your Best Life Now

5
The Reality of Visitations

Visitations cause stress for children because they are shuttled between different homes, with different rules, expectations, and values--or there is confusion about who is in charge when you and their using parent are together during supervised visits.

Sober parents and relative caregivers say they too are frustrated, and often feel powerless, because of dictates from foster services, family courts, or because they are parenting without any binding legal custody and/or guardianship arrangement. They compare visitations to being in a pressure cooker, and transition days/times like walking on eggshells.

Reality

Gregory S. Forman, a family law attorney and certified family court mediator wrote, "If I were a family court judge every alcoholic parent would be given a stark choice: alcohol or your children. If the parent chose alcohol, he or she would not receive court-ordered visitation…if they choose visitation they would be ordered not to drink *period.*"[23] Sadly, that's not reality. Reality is that separating kids from a drinking, or drug using, parent is typically a long, messy process. By necessity you become an investigator, documenter, and whistle blower while supervising visits or, at least, monitoring the pick-ups and drop offs. You patch kids together who are falling apart both before they go, and after they return.

State laws reflect the premise that birth parents have a legal right to spend time with their children on a regular basis unless they are an imminent danger to their son or daughter. Caseworkers and judges make visitation decisions that will have life-long impact for your kids, or grandkids, based on legal precedence and filtered facts. However painful, if the state has guardianship, or you are going through a legal custody battle, you have to walk through the child protection agency or court hoops until the using parent proves to be a serious risk or they voluntarily surrender their right to visitations. If you have custody, but it's an informal arrangement with an alcoholic or addict, you really do need to talk to an attorney to discover your options based on your specific situation.

In the meantime, try to *think of visitations as a bridge to get from where you are, to where you want to be. Not all bridges are permanent, but all bridges can be useful.* There is always a chance that your grown son, daughter, or soon-to-be ex will stop using permanently and can be trusted to be part of their kid's lives, or more likely the opposite, that they cannot. The fact that you feel like a hostage to their whims and/or the system's bureaucracy doesn't count for anything legally, so suck it up and keep on, keeping on.

The benefit and the pain of visitations is that kids eventually see their parent(s) for who they are...

Susi, now a twenty-eight year-old college graduate, had a mother who used drugs to "self-medicate for her undiagnosed bipolar condition." Her parents divorced when she was in the second grade. "At first I wanted contact, but the more I had the worse I'd feel. I was sad, not happy. My mom would call and say she was picking me up at school at two, and I'd wait outside on the steps, but she wouldn't show up. I then had to call my grandparents, who I lived with off and on, to come get me. In the third grade, I didn't want to see her anymore. I didn't trust her." Some children need to see that their using parent is okay. Some want to tell their mom or dad that they love them, while hoping they will be told the same. Others end up using visits as a way of letting go, or making sure that their addicted parent knows that they are mad at them, sad, or hate them. Most have mixed feelings. Many want no contact. Keep remembering the visitation bridge is serving its purpose; your role is to make sure the toll isn't too high by just being there for your children and grandchildren.

Control what you can

Oregon therapist, Heather McIntosh, talked about visitation problems at a 2014 Relative Caregiver's Retreat, *"The parent coming back and forth continues trauma. The trauma never stops. Take a day or two to process your own trauma, not just the kids' trauma. It's important to validate that to yourself, and find a peaceful place."* This means you need a friend, counselor, or both, to talk with because your feelings regarding the addict also keep being stirred up. Seeing them, and being forced to deal with the fallout when their kids are screaming, or crying, or cutting can be devastating.

Make the time together with their parent as peaceful as possible for the little ones, but don't lose yourself in the deal. Schedule visitations for days, times, and places that best fit into the children's and your schedules, not the addict's, and are scenarios that your heart can handle. *Tears spill down my face now, just as they did twenty plus years ago, when Chad was two years old and my daughter had weekly visitations with him at a local state child protection office. I would take off of work each week to go pick up Brandy and then be in the room playing with Chad, or just watching the two interact. The hardest part was helping him put on his jacket at the end of each of those visits, and giv-*

ing his little hand to the transportation driver who drove him back to the foster home. I will never forget the sight of Chad walking slowly toward the door. I never turned away, or left, until he did--just to be there in case he looked back. After I dropped off Brandy, I'd pull over to the curb somewhere and sob. Some pieces of your heart once broken just stay broken.

If you supervise visits but want your weekends free, then try to make it happen. It may mean agreeing to one Saturday, or Sunday, each month at your place for four hours, with an hour mid-week play date at McDonald's in-between. It could be getting together Tuesday afternoons at a supervising agency, or for an hour after cheerleading practice Friday nights while your daughter, or granddaughter, and her dad walk the track and you read in the bleachers. If you try something and it isn't working, then regroup—even if it means going back to court, or negotiating a new plan with the using parent, or a caseworker.

If mom or dad are *habitually late* wait fifteen minutes for supervised, and an hour for unsupervised, and then leave, or don't answer the door if they show up. Do not reschedule for 'late' or 'no shows'. Addicts have excuses for why they cannot come, or were not there on time. Their car won't start; they had to work overtime. They are out of gas, or did not get paid and couldn't take their son to play paintball as they promised. Creative thinking on their part but usually untrue, or a result of poor choices. Don't over-react when you eventually connect. Calmly, but firmly, tell them that you waited and then moved onto plan B but that you'll see them during their next scheduled visit. Don't offer additional explanation or engage in arguments. Keep a running log of dates, times, comments, and kids' reactions.

Safety

Child abduction, domestic violence, child abuse, theft, and the introducing of drugs or alcohol to progeny can occur during any visitation. *If you feel there is risk, control every variable that you possibly can.* Meet only in public parks, malls, and pizza parlors to provide some sense of normalcy and activities for the kids, with increased personal security for everyone. There are agencies, and in some cities private businesses, that will monitor visits. Setting up appointments and paying service fees should be the addict's responsibility. If they have the time and money for drugs, or drinking, they can make visits happen.

When getting together in your home is the best option but you feel threatened or overwhelmed, ask a family member or acquaintance to oversee the visits, or be there with you. If it appears that the user has been drinking, or using drugs, do not let them in. Tell them to wait outside or leave, but tell them that if they stay you are calling the police. Then do it. Even if the police take no action, the call becomes a matter of record. *Never allow anyone but the family member inside your home unless you know and trust him, or her.* You have no idea what strangers will do. They could assault you or the children, plan future break-ins, or they may keep the alcoholic in line but why chance it?

Proving that your son, daughter, or prior partner uses drugs or alcohol during a time frame (typically defined as 24-hours before or during a visit) that could threaten minors' safety rests on your shoulders. Things are more complicated in states with legalized drug use so talk to a lawyer in advance and develop a 'what if' plan. Brandy once suggested buying a home drug test and asking them to, "Pee on the spot" but to, "do it politely away from the kids. If they throw a fit, then something's going on...you can tell a lot from body language. You then have to decide how to terminate the visitation. You have to think about your safety. I'm not sure if you can legally terminate a court-ordered visit." Not a bad suggestion, but you risk physical confrontation, and the kids will see you as 'the bad guy' regardless of the outcome. Forman actually suggested that anyone who agreed to not use, and tests positive, be found in contempt of court. Great idea, but truthfully you'll be lucky to get visits moved from unsupervised to supervised, or temporarily suspended. *Many alcoholics and addicts eventually destroy their own chances for continuing visitations by not showing up, or showing up under the influence too many times.*

Don't set kids up

Another reason for 'parent only' supervised visits (you can't control who is with the alcoholic for unsupervised visits unless their behavior is endangering and then the third party requiring the visits will have to determine what action to take and how to enforce it) is to keep kids, not the alcoholic's friends, the center of attention. When Brandy was single, and Chad first lived with me, she'd bring a boyfriend and the two of them would all but sit on each other's laps; Chad was like a prop, not a player. The paroled felon asked me to use my shower—and from then on I told Brandy to visit alone.

By the time Chad was in the fifth grade, Brandy was married and living several hours away. Chad and I traveled to see her, and his half-sisters, at their apartment. Brandy's attention was rightly split between the four siblings. Afterwards he seemed down, so I asked him if he liked visiting his mom. His response was, **"I like to see her. Happy, but sometimes I feel when I do go see her I get a little ignored. That's all I can say."** A few years ago Chad added, **"It's still the case."** Today, as a young adult, he better understands the dynamics when a using or sober addict has other children living with them. **"The child who comes for a "visitation" is ignored in some way. They are the outcast. The alcoholic probably won't pick up on it, and their siblings don't get it. The influence, and connectivity, that the addict has over the kids living with them is a lot more than with the one that isn't, unless the separation has just happened."**

Don't allow addicts to participate in field trips, birthday parties, graduations, and other special events unless they occur during a regularly scheduled visit and it is an event that you have no control over. You can't stop the bio-parent, without a restraining order, from showing up at public venues such as lacrosse games or chess tournaments, or even a graduation if they snag a ticket or it's open seating; however, don't mention the occasion in advance, facilitate attendance, or include them in your plans for afterwards. "No," is a complete sentence. "This is our day," a truthful response. Adolescents shouldn't have to worry if mom will be high, or dad won't be there after promising he would. Also, you are parenting—they are visiting. You deserve a few of the parenting highs because there are more than enough lows due to the addict.

Unsupervised visits

When planning visitations concentrate on the purpose—child/ parent connection—not on problems. Talk with, not at, the non-custodial birth parent. Try to agree on ground rules, or resolve problems, when children aren't present. *Choose your battles.* What junk food youth are allowed to eat or when they shower is not crucial, but appropriate activities or maintaining pick-up and drop off schedules, and alcohol free visits are battle-worthy. *Look for 'work-arounds'* when possible, such as negotiating earlier return times during the school year if your son, daughter, or grandkids aren't getting enough sleep or homework isn't getting done. Using the same logic, keep your opinion to yourself if they come home with a lot of 'things' that you think are a waste of money—unless you previously said 'no' to something for a valid reason other than you can't afford it while being the responsible bill payer. Good time to mention that late, or non-payment of, child support is a separate issue better discussed another time; also, you cannot withhold visitations because of non-compliance.

Tactfully suggest activities that enhance the children's lives rather than having them cooped up in an apartment watching TV or playing video games all weekend. Libby promoted scouting activities because her sons and ex-husband loved camping and working on projects for badges. The organization's zero tolerance for alcohol gave her an added sense of peace. She allowed her ex to fly with the kids across the country every summer for a two-week vacation with his parents. The parents monitored for sobriety and chaperoned everyone's downtime, as well as oversaw activities. It was a win-win for everyone.

Don't compromise on critical issues. No unplanned out-of-state travel, sexual activity of any kind with anyone, or drug/alcohol use. *If anything illegal does happen call the police immediately.* One grandmother confided that her teenage granddaughter came home with semen on her underwear. When questioned, the girl said she slept in her dad's bed but "nothing happened". The grandmother washed her granddaughter's clothes and had the girl take a shower, so there was no evidence to collaborate the story. *If something upsetting occurs call the caseworker, and rapidly escalate the issue up the chain of command if you don't get immediate action.* An aunt, who has court ordered visitations, made a seven-year-old boy strip in front of her, and although she didn't touch him, she made him self-conscious with her staring. Illegal? Don't know, but it was reported and was being looked into by the caseworker when I heard the story. If something makes you uncomfortable talk to your attorney, or possibly the state attorney general. The worst that can happen is that you get information, and at the same time create that paper trail we keep mentioning.

Phone calls, texts, emails, and social network communication, are "visitations" and should be limited, supervised, or prohibited depending on visitation agreements. Blocking phone numbers, or email addresses, is basically useless because birthparents, and their kids, can use other people's phones, have multiple social personas and will always be a step ahead of you in discovering the 'newest' digital communication apps. Chapter fourteen tells you how to check phones, computers and other technology to keep tweens and teens safe, and your relationship in tact.

More about trust

Trust is critical to all relationships, and any type of contact with birth parents means they continue impacting their kids. Staying in touch with Brandy, albeit sparingly except for hers and Chad's late night clandestine phone calls, caused huge problems. In high school Chad wrote, "Respect. Trust. In today's society, we don't think of how these could be lost or broken, or even how much they mean. Trust means so much, and when it's gone it's gone for good. Zip, pow, gone. Trust is built up over time, but can be broken in an instant or over multiple instances and time.

Brandy lost all of my trust and she will never, ever earn it back. See, she made a promise with me that she would never do anything to hurt me again. This promise made it through many years, until summer '07. During that summer, Brandy 'lost' her job and basically disappeared from my life. She did come back after many incidents, and events, that I do not wish to talk about. She hurt me.

Trust with kids like me, is a big issue. If I can't trust you, I can't be around you. So I guess the point I'm trying to make is that kids who have gone through horrible things, need to have trust in other people. Trust is vital to living."

More recently he added, "Kids learn from what happens. So when they get attached and their parent randomly goes away, they think every good friend, or people they date, will do that too."

At different times, Brandy was both a perpetrator and a victim in the visitation triangle, telling me, *"Time after time my 'ex' [Ryan] would call from out-of-town and tell our three daughters that he would be there that weekend. Then he wouldn't call, or show up, and I had to hear, 'Where's daddy? What's he doing? Why aren't we more important than anything else to him?' It was heart-wrenching and disgusting. Then I started drinking and became the unreliable parent; their dad did the right thing by taking the girls. I was pissed then, but he did absolutely the right thing."* I agree.

When Chad was little, Brandy was the "no show." I still have a whale whistle he bought for her when we visited 'Keiko' the star of his favorite childhood movie *Free Willy,* and I have the vivid memory of his tears when she didn't call, or come over, on the day he planned to give it to her. I learned not to tell Chad in advance about plans involving Brandy, and encouraged him to make, or buy things, for other family members instead. "She still does not understand the damage she did," says my husband, "but she was not here to see, so she could not understand. With her daughters there's no excuse."

His junior year, Chad had an English assignment to list 100 things about himself; most concerned his birthparents, death, and depression. "1. Every tear I cry is dry; #25 I listen to a lot of death metal, progressive death metal, brutal death metal, screamo; #59 Sometimes I do wish that I was dead; #60 I used to talk to my birth mom everyday and tell her everything; #61 I haven't talked to my birth mom in over eight months; #68 My dad abused me because he was an alcoholic and, #83 I sometimes wonder why we have a God that gives us so much choice that our mistakes can ruin other peoples lives, and leave them with no choices".

69

Post visitation havoc

Every visit has repercussions—positive and negative. If you ask an older kid how an unsupervised visit went, they'll probably respond, "fine", "whatever", or something equally lame. However, if they are slamming doors, not talking, shoving their parent's picture in a drawer, or being disrespectful when you are trying to settle them back into a routine, you know better. Younger ones may cry, run around, yell, or start talking about how they hate their parent or hate you. Some want to go live with "mommy". *Before the next visit, talk to kids about setting up a transition time (*fifteen to sixty minutes depending on their age and your schedule) to help them transition when they return from every visit, regardless if it is a Disney dream day, a disaster, or something in-between. During this time they can snack, watch cartoons, hang out in their room, play video games, unpack, or call friends. Let them know you love them, and will be there to talk with them if they choose, but that you won't bug them about the visit, tomorrow's school work, chores, or getting ready for bed. After transition time resume your household's normal routine, but hold off on mommy/daddy questions.

Teens naturally turn to peers or other adults with their confidences…it's part of growing up so don't be alarmed if they don't volunteer information. Regardless of age, if they are typically moody or out of control after visitations and they go to counseling, schedule appointments for the next day when possible. This gives them a safe adult to confide in without feeling that they are betraying their birth mom or dad, or hurting you. Email, text, or ask their counselor when you arrive to be part of the first few minutes of the session if something monumental happened during, or as a result of, the visit. The therapist can then zero in on whatever it is that is turning your household upside down.

If counseling isn't an option, wait a day or two to see if they come to you. During that time concentrate on relationship building, however, don't ignore bad behavior. A firm, "I know you are upset about something that happened at your mother's place, but hitting is not acceptable," or "Ignacio why don't you go outside and slam a tennis ball rather than stay inside slamming drawers and risk breaking something you care about?" should do it. Interestingly, researchers say it takes about five positive comments for every negative one.[24] So while delving into what happened, and their subsequent feelings, go back to the visitation first and point out the things they handled well. If you need to talk about their interim behavior, try to give them kudos whenever you honestly can. Small steps of improvement—not punching the wall, or swearing, or terrorizing their younger siblings are all things to celebrate even in the midst of tears, sulking, or silence.

Don't make kids choose

Let kids love both you and their using birth parent; it's not a competition. Simple comments such as, "That's a great card you made for your mom," or "would you like to hug your dad goodbye?" are all that's necessary. Never criticize the parent as a person, and sparingly (hard to do) comment on their behavior in a constructive and non-threatening manner. Saying, "We have different memories, and feelings, toward your mom and that's okay," may help, but older kids will more likely personalize whatever you say and try to turn it back on you. When Pepper, Chad's 16-year-old half-sister, lived with us for a few months last year we had a lot of discussions. She said she cried while watching a movie in health class that showed how an addicted dad treated his family—and then she tried to justify similar actions by her dad! She argued that no one gave Ryan a break or help when he needed it, rejecting—even while acknowledging—the truth. *She was defensive and defending. Talking or texting Brandy and her old friends multiple times that day, and every day, didn't help. They told her what she wanted to hear, and in the end she wanted to go back to her old lifestyle.*

When parents tell lies like, "You're coming to live with me," confront immediately. Talk to the kiddos, "Remember the judge said you will live with grandpa and me, not your mom." Next time you are altogether, and this is crucial if you want the behavior to stop because most addicts try to avoid confrontation, ask the adult, "Before you start the movie (or leave for the weekend), I just want to make sure we all understand that (use child/grandchild's name) is going to live with me, not you—right mom (and look directly at her)?"

Involve youth in planning whenever possible. Give choices acceptable to you such as, "Do you want to ask your mom to go with us for pizza? Would you rather see your dad here, or at the park? I wish you wouldn't write to your dad while he's in jail, but if you'll show me his letters and your responses, unless there is something that may hurt you or endanger our family, I'll allow it. Deal?" Seriously consider their suggestions, even if you have to discuss and modify them, otherwise they'll think it's you against their parent, or you against their parent and them.

Don't treat kids as messengers or spies. Young ones will spill their guts without prompting, middle and high schoolers not so much. All are more likely to tell you things about their parent, while doing things they like, so go for a milkshake, play a video game, paint each other's toenails, or shoot hoops. Chad usually shared what was bothering him but waited until bedtime; we had a lot of long, late night chats but it was worth it. "☺" adds Chad.

Help kids get help

Make sure your children or grandchildren know their last name (and yours if different), your phone number, how to use both cell and landline phones, the city where you live, and who they can ask for help if they are abducted, or left alone during an unsupervised visitation.

It's important to teach kids how to be safe, and who they can safely approach when you aren't with them. Teach them that police, firemen, teachers, military, and friends' parents are there to help in an emergency or if they are afraid. If a phone isn't available, your kids need to know that it's okay to run outside and find a neighbor who can help them. Teach your kids how to dial 911 and make sure they know what it's for. If Chad had known to call 911 or talk to a neighbor in an adjoining apartment when Donald drank and passed out—both doable at age three--Chad could have been removed much sooner.

Discuss possible scenarios. For example you might say, "If dad colors your hair and will not let you call me, or mom takes you on a trip that I didn't tell you about then talk to a policeman, mother with kids, store clerk, or teacher. Don't worry if your mother/father says they'll hurt me; I can take care of myself." Tell youngsters to use the words, "*The judge says* I should live with my grandpa, not my dad." Phrases like *the judge says* are not normal kid talk and command attention. Tell them what to do if a parent is drunk, if there are drugs or needles around, no food for meals, or there are strangers in the home who scare, or touch, them inappropriately. *Role-play responses.*

Abductions happen. If a parent is more than an hour late in returning from an outing, or takes your child without permission, call the police immediately who can issue an amber alert. After the first twenty-four hours the chances of recovery drop dramatically so don't be afraid of embarrassing yourself if it turns out to be a false alarm. Keep, in an easy-to-access spot, the make, license number, year, and color of the car the user owns along with names and numbers of bosses or friends. Include recent face shots of children and their parent, as well as, children's dental records, custodial orders, and social security numbers. As a precaution, block passport applications for minors by filing the necessary paperwork with the Federal

Immigration Services. Also, be extra vigilant if the parent quits their job or starts selling possessions.

If the kids you are parenting show symptoms of emotional overload or behavior problems, such as regressing to wetting the bed again, refusing to take their parent's calls, or their grades drop, try to stop unsupervised visits until things are sorted out. It could be they are hurt or angry over something small; or it could be they were asked to use, steal, or be a go-between for drug deals. They could have been molested, or it could be nothing more than they are growing up and they'd rather be with their friends.

Final thoughts

When negotiating visitation terms ask for 'reasonable and seasonable' language instead of specifics such as the 'first and third weekends and alternating holidays'. This saves you from having to go back to court, or risk being in contempt, if the addict relapses or the kids aren't handling the visits well and you need to make adjustments. It still puts the burden of acting responsible and justifying, if challenged, changes to the number, supervision, or duration of visits on you so document, document, and document.

Don't share personal details about children with non-custodial parents unless you are doing so in lieu of visitations. Some addicts/alcoholics will agree, especially if visits don't go well, to your sending them pictures and progress letters in place of visits (like an open adoption). Get their consent in writing. Have it witnessed by a neutral third party if possible and file with the court to have visitations modified, eliminated or even start the process to revoke parental rights. Make sure the parent sees an attorney—even if you have to pay the attorney they choose directly—to avoid their coming back years later and saying their rights weren't explained to them, or they signed under duress. *If you do adopt or get sole custody and guardianship without legally mandated visitations don't, out of misguided guilt or sympathy, allow visits. Precedents, however well intentioned, can come back to bite you.*

If your child lives in the world, your child will be exposed to the world...even though kids don't have the mental capacity or maturity level that we have to deal with it.

James Lehman, MSW, Empoweringparents.com

6
Behind Bar Visitations

For little kids, I think, it's a really big deal for them to see their incarcerated birth parent. Yeah, they're in a bad place but kids don't understand that, and seeing that their mom or dad still exists is important. When they are older then it depends entirely on relationships, and if they want to go. You have to ask yourself, "Who is this visit helping and who is it hurting?"

The courts have repeatedly upheld that incarcerated parents have a right to see their children. Visits can alleviate a son or daughter's fears and promote bonding; however, I'm doubling down on my advice to break the ties sooner, rather than later. Seeing dad through a visiting screen, or mom in handcuffs or shackles, can also add new layers of fear, anxiety, shame, embarrassment, or uncertainty for already struggling kids. *"We underwent a body search whenever we visited my father... We had to identify him by a number. I felt so isolated and alone... I couldn't share my pain and shame with my friends,"* said Laura Kaeppeler, a recent Miss America.[25]

The addict landed themself in jail and nothing you do, or don't do, will compel them to use their time behind bars, or after release, constructively. That is up to them. In a study of 16,420 Minnesota inmates, released between 2003 and 2007, visits from the children of inmates helped reduce recidivism by 9% or less.[26]

On the other hand, children seeing their parents in prison are often negatively impacted, harming them now and possibly for life. Many caregivers say that the days following prison visits can be very, very difficult, because kids are angry, sad, or mixed up, and trying to sort out their feelings. Teachers in one research study, "Reported that students often had trouble concentrating in school following weekend visits with their incarcerated parents. Teachers tended to have made more positive comments about the effects of mail contact between students and their incarcerated parents."[27]

You have options: no visits, one visit for closure, a limited number of visits, or regular scheduled on-going visits. You can also schedule the children to 'visit' via phone, Skype, or letter only. Supervise alternatives as closely as you would face-to-face meetings, monitoring what is said, and shutting them down if the child appears overwhelmed.

For connection without physical contact Dr. Michelle Watson, a private practice counselor and author of, *Dad, Here's What I Really Need from You: A Guide For Connecting with Your Daughter's Heart* made the following suggestion when I was interviewing her (she doesn't talk about prison in her book). Ask the incarcerated dad "to write down their prayers, dreams, scripture promises, and/or wishes for their daughter. It will serve as a time capsule for her when she is more mature. Just to know that her dad was ACTUALLY thinking about her at various times in their life could go far in building a bridge between them in the future." This could work equally well for moms/dads and sons/daughters in any combination. It could also help the parent process their feelings and possibly change their life.

Court orders are the exception

If there are court-ordered prison visits then again, regardless of your or the minor's feelings, you have to obey unless you can convince a judge that doing so causes, or would cause, the child substantial harm. Ask everyone, but especially teachers, social workers and counselors who have frequent contact with your child, to write down their observations pre and post visitations. Keeping track of incidents and/or reactions—good and bad--is essential. Eventually, you'll have the proof you need to change the court's mind, or you will change yours.

If you and the kids are going...

Most facilities have their own website for downloading forms, checking out visiting days and times, and finding other pertinent information. Background checks are required for everyone wanting to visit and some states charge a one-time non-refundable service fee. If you pass the background check but the inmate doesn't put you on their approved visitor list, you won't get in. Years ago Brandy told me, *"When I was serving time, it was at a coed minimum security facility that was dorm style, not cells. Visitors met in the cafeteria and each prisoner was at their own table. You didn't know who would be sitting next to you on visiting days. There was a woman at the time, in a wheel chair, who murdered her own kids. Sometimes, depending on the mindset and maturity of the children and why you are there, yeah visits are okay. When I was drinking I wouldn't have wanted it. I was ashamed. I'm kind of wishy-washy about kids going to prison, but if they are older and can make up their own mind, they need to be part of the decision. If a teenager thinks crime and jail is cool, absolutely not. If they're angry with me as a parent and they need to get things off their chest, yes. If they want to let a parent know they're there for them, that's okay."* Before her comments I incorrectly assumed she'd want her family to visit, and that medium or low security prisons housed less violent criminals.

Once approved, and the paper work is completed, you may need to make a reservation because the number of visitors allowed in a facility, and the number of visitors with any one inmate at a given time, can be limited. *Go alone the first time.* Always allow more time than you think necessary in case of traffic, parking, and processing problems. If you arrive late, you will be turned away. The initial meeting could be awkward but it's your opportunity to say the things that are personal between you two, or inappropriate for kids to hear. If you are undecided, or concerned, about bringing their sons/daughters to prison say so up front. *Listen with your heart, but filter through your brain.*

Each of you needs to talk about your expectations, boundaries, and concerns regarding future visits. Toddlers will fidget. Infants will cry. Preteens and high school students may sulk or sneer, be shy, angry, or withdrawn. Children are honest and curious creatures. They will probably ask questions or make comments that can be hurtful, embarrassing, sad, or amusing. Remarks about changes in their parent's looks, parenting role, or the facility's rules including, "Why can't I sit on your lap, daddy?" or "Dude you can't make me do anything," aren't unusual.

If anything you see or hear makes you uneasy, or you are still undecided about taking the kids, then call a mentor, friend, family member, or counselor before you make a decision. Others who are not as emotionally involved, may be able to provide just the perspective you need. If you change your mind from "yes" to "no", or vice versa, don't apologize. Pat yourself on the back for having made a tough decision without causing the children false hope, or unnecessary anxiety, during the process.

You and the kids

If you are taking the kids, regardless of why—and sometimes it may be simply to give a grandchild, son or daughter closure-

-then start by talking logistics and feelings. Discuss barbed wire, armed guards, metal detectors, or the fact that they will be talking by phone or video feed if that's the case. For tiny ones, wait until you are almost there and then say something like, "We're going to see mom today. She won't be able to run and play, or come home with us, but it will be good to see her." I was very little when Brandy was in state prison and mom and I have no idea if she was in jail later on when she relapsed and became an alcoholic. I didn't miss her when I was three and never noticed that she wasn't around.

Adolescents are picky about how they look so have them check the dress code online, even if you already know it, so you aren't the bad guy. Girls will likely resent having to wear longer, and looser, dresses and shorts than they are used to, or no underwire, bras. Boys who like Levis™ or sagging shorts probably won't be happy about having to wear pants that aren't denim, don't have studs, or are not excessively baggy. Neither sex can wear the same colors, or styles, as the staff or inmates' uniforms. Check restrictions carefully because they are strictly enforced.

I recently spoke at a men's maximum-security penitentiary as part of my Christian writer group's outreach. The temperature was hovering close to one hundred and the air conditioning, I knew, was old and weak. By the time I'd eliminated everything that would be too hot, too dressy, too casual, or too revealing I was down to a bright turquoise shirt, with rolled up long sleeves, and white pants. It never dawned on me that my shirt would be considered blue, which is taboo because inmates frequently wear chambray shirts. The guards wouldn't let me in. Thanks to the kindness of a stranger in the lobby who had a X-large men's black T-shirt in his car, that he gave me, I got in but ironically black was the color of T-shirts the inmates were wearing that night! Mine had a "Celebrate Recovery" slogan across the front and it looked like an oversized sleep shirt on me—so I told the men that I was a walking commercial. Got a lot of laughs, but I wouldn't want your family to be turned away, so if in doubt ask before leaving home.

Other items typically prohibited include hoodies, belts, tobacco products, electronic devices, and certain types or excessive amounts of jewelry, gang colors/symbols, t-shirts with drug/ alcohol or offensive sayings, most types of boots, as well as non-prescription sunglasses. If your religion requires hijabs, yarmulkes, or other types of special clothing, anticipate more invasive searches. Explain that guards look for contraband and anything that could be used as a weapon, for everyone's safety. Make sure the young ones understand that smuggling contraband going in, or coming out, will get them in big trouble.

Encourage kids to *be honest* with their parent about their feelings and discuss with them how feeling sad, mad, scared, excited, happy, or confused is natural because of what has, and is, happening to them. Then remind yourself that you cannot protect them from the reality of where their parent is, what their parent says, or prison/jail life in general. *Don't jump in prematurely, trying to smooth things over, unless a child is in over their head.* If you're taking them to visit their parent—let them visit! I'm guessing that you want them to see the reality of their mom/dad's choices, so don't mess with reality.

Tweens and teens—especially if they have recently come to live with you—may be very conflicted and feel protective of their mom or so don't try to force the conversation or push emotional buttons. There will be communication and relationship successes and failures, and from each they will learn. Their parents will also. However, for children of all ages, establish a code word that tells you if they want to leave but want it to appear that you are the one terminating the visit. Don't make "life lesson" comments after you leave, but be open and willing to let them vent, or withdraw inside themselves to think. There will be plenty of time and opportunities over next few days, and weeks, to help them work through what transpired.

Plan well, stress less on visiting day

The following is a list of things, in no particular order, that others have shared:

➤ If you have limited money for gas, bus fare, meals, or hotels ask government agencies, community/private, or faith-sponsored groups for help or referrals to others who can help you. The Internet is also a source of information, for example, Washington State's Department of Corrections' (DOCC) website lists three volunteer run transportation possibilities. While the Prison Society in Pennsylvania offers $40 bus service, per person, from Philadelphia's 30th street station to all but four state correctional institutions. New York's DOCC promotes free bus service for families living in several larger cities. And volunteer 'host families', in limited communities throughout the U.S., make available places for kids to stay temporarily so they can be closer to their incarcerated parent—especially during school breaks.[28]

➤ *There are in-facility programs helping children and incarcerated parents interact.* Favorites include week-long summer youth camps, run by volunteers at select facilities in Maryland and North Carolina, providing daily parent/child visits followed by typical camp activities at near-by campgrounds during off hours. Many prisons offer year-round reading or scouting programs. *Note: jails are typically less child-friendly than prisons because they tend to house transient and short-term offenders.*

➤ For security, or other reasons, visiting times may be shorten or cancelled, so always check the website before leaving home. Avoid meal and prisoner head-count times when delays typically occur; select only days and times when the inmate is not scheduled to work or be in class or you'll probably end up not getting to see them.

➤ Place baby bottles, diapers, change of clothes, or any other infant necessities in clear zip lock bags. Many sites require babies and young girls to have leggings under dresses, due to the presence of sex offenders.

➤ Some places require debit or credit cards; others only accept cash for vending machines as well as for lockers for storing car keys and other personal belongings. Money for inmates' use must be placed in their personal accounts—no cash is allowed in their possession.

➤ Each visitor (except infants and elementary students who need their own social security card and/or birth certificate) has to show government/school issued picture ID. It will be held by guards and returned when you exit secured areas.

➤ Young people get bored waiting and keeping them entertained without electronics can be challenging. Bring books, games or homework to keep them occupied in waiting rooms.

➤ Eat before going or take meals/snacks that can be consumed in transit.

➤ Leave life-sustaining prescription medications that could be needed while visiting in their original container with the pharmaceutical label. Advise staff at check in so meds are not confiscated, or your visit terminated.

➤ Hide extra cash, credit cards, and electronics in out-of-sight areas of your car *before* parking at the jail or prison, or leave them home. Break-ins occur even in secured lots. Searches of vehicles by staff, including drug-sniffing dogs, are possible.

On family visiting days

Try to relax; you've done what you could so now go with the flow. If kids are talkative on the drive there, ask if they have any questions or concerns; if they are quiet, don't worry. If they are crabby—eat chocolate. Seriously, they will be okay because you are there with them. **It may not always be you that they child wants to be there with them. It may be a friend's mom or dad, your husband, your boyfriend, or even just a friend that they need for the drive there and back. Just make sure that your child/ grandchild is put first over the person they are going to see, and prepare them for whatever may happen.**

In closing

School counselors and caseworkers often know about *opportunities for children of incarcerated parents* whether they are in touch, or not, with their mom or dad. Just being with other youth, living with similar situations and experiencing similar feelings, can be helpful for kids. The people, running these programs, are trained staff or dedicated volunteers. The structure tends to be in-school support groups, on-going after-school care combined with planned activities, or single events such as retreats and special trainings focused on skill building or fun. Leadership, make-up, resume creation/job interviewing, and college preparation classes are popular with older youth. Holiday events, such as Christmas parties and themed summer camps focusing on sports, computers, Lego™ building and music or science themes are popular with younger children. *New Hope* in Oklahoma and *Children of Promise* in Brooklyn, New York offer two kid-centered activity resources that we heard about through referrals.

Because addicts tend to be introspective and remorseful when incarcerated, and relapse after release, be wary of making future plans. If the released user starts drinking or using drugs again, you will be the one picking up the pieces. "Let's wait and see," is a reasonable response. *Doing a good thing at the wrong time, or for the wrong reasons, seldom results in a happy ending.*

Who knew that love for your family can bring you to your knees.

Connie Schultz

7
'Heart Smart' Holidays

Just say, "No". "No, you can't have Aiden on his birthday, it's not your regular visitation day." "No, you can't come for Passover, or Christmas, or birthdays; you ruined the last two years." "No, I don't feel guilty." Say it to yourself. Say it to the addict. Then walk away, hang up, or change the subject. Don't debate it. Don't react. Just move on.

I took the following defining words, and some of the ideas in each bulletin point from a Rick Warren 'Daily Hope' message[29], but I'm using them here in an entirely different context—he was talking faith, I'm talking drugs and booze.

- **Doubt.** Stop thinking, 'what if'. What if the addict commits suicide, or overdoses? What if my grandkids/kids hate me for not letting them see their dad? *Well, what if they don't? What if your actions actually save the alcoholic's life? What if an addict-free holiday gives the rest of the family happy memories and teaches them how to be mama or daddy to their kids?*
- **Discouragement.** You tell yourself nothing will change. You're right; nothing will change unless you want it to, and then make it happen.

- **Delay.** It's easy to say, "I'll make a decision tomorrow," and then the next holiday is here, with disaster repeating itself. If everyone in your family knows before hand what changes to expect—they'll handle it. They'll probably thank you.
- **Difficulty.** Stop asking, "Why is this so hard?" and tell yourself instead, "I can do hard."
- **Depression.** "It's not worth it. " You are wrong. The life of a child is always worth sacrifice and emotional risk. Tough love needs to be directed at yourself, as well as, the user.

"It may be extremely difficult, but families must come to peace with the idea that an addicted family member often needs to reach a personal low to finally make a change and accept recovery", says Robert W. Mooney, M.D. *Maybe being alone for holidays will give them the low that finally makes them want to do the work to get better.* "Nobody will ever get sober without some sort of trouble—legal, financial, marital—that promotes the opportunity for recovery," he says. "Being able to release with love without feeling guilt is important."[30]

You are the children's buffer

Do not count on addicts for holidays. The family at your house, that's the family you want to be with. It causes more hurt to try to revolve the day around a user and have them be a 'no show', or have them come and it not be that amazing. Put your child/grandchild first! Make it fun for them, and make sure it looks like you are having fun too. Create an atmosphere that is family oriented to the people that are there and not the one person missing.

For years, Chad and I decorated cookies at Christmas; then he lost interest. I chalked it up to his growing up, and didn't think anything more about it until a few years ago when he was home from college at winter break. I suggested he bring Jessica over and we make cookies. He said he was helping her family bake goodies later that week, but it wasn't fun anymore, **"Not since Brandy didn't show up that one year."** As it turned out, they had a great time making flour messes and decorating dinosaurs and buffalos (okay, so that is a weird winter holiday design). A week later Chad initiated their coming over to our house to decorate cookies, and watch my favorite holiday movie.

It took years of counseling and working through these types of hurts for Chad—and there were a lot more anchored to holidays--to recognize the root cause, and to readily share his feelings with me. I love that he now has the confidence to build his future on his choices and recent experiences, not on baggage left over from his birthparents.

The addict or alcoholic's siblings

Life moves on. Your other grown, or nearly grown, sons and daughters are now likely trying to protect you, protect their nieces and nephews, and most importantly, protect their own spouse and kids. They've been through no booze get-togethers where everyone but their alcoholic brother was sober, and empty medicine cabinet holidays when their addicted sister stole Aunt Carol's pills out of her purse or showed up after snorting a line. They've tried to talk over their sibling's face plants at the dinner table, and sucked up their own tears as the addict exploded over something minor and ruined yet another holiday.

Emotions are always on edge at the holidays because we've been conditioned to buy into perfect 'Hallmark" fantasies. Holidays for siblings are more often horror days. The really disturbing thing is that these young adults have probably seen a lot of things that you don't even know about if they are close in age to the user. They arrive for family get-togethers carrying their personal and collective baggage.

"He had friends over and they'd been drinking. I came into the living room, it was dark with the lights off, and I just started screaming and crying...I thought he was dead," says Patty a single twenty-something mom who lives in Minnesota and discovered her brother, Mike, when he tried to commit suicide by hanging himself. She was sixteen, and he was a senior in high school. Not breathing when she cut him down, Mike quickly regained consciousness after hitting the floor and then went to bed saying, "It was no big deal." Patty told him it was a "big deal" and that he needed to tell their parents about his use of pot, drinking, and the suicide attempt when they returned from a weekend trip. She stayed awake for 48-hours; Mike slept and did not say anything to their mom or dad. So Patty called her aunt and, for the first time ever, shared her burden with an adult family member.

Ten years later Patty explains, *"I hated Mike in high school and could not wait to go away to college. Mike was an angry drunk. I always had to clean up after him, kick his friends out.*

They were mean to me, and he hit on my best friends. I knew and didn't tell my parents because he didn't want me to; I felt it was his place to tell them. My biggest regret is that I didn't tell my parents sooner and they could have gotten him help." She feels sorry for her brother, but says he uses his depression and threatens suicide to manipulate their mom. *"I finally yelled, 'Let me go get you a rope.' I was at the end of mine."* He's never threatened their mother with it again.

Jessie, Mike's younger sister by seven years, has different memories and regrets, *"The first time I drank it wasn't with Mike, but the first time I did drugs, the summer between fifth and sixth grade, it was with him. He said, 'Want to go get high?' and I said 'sure.'"* Jessie ended up in rehab four years later. I first interviewed her when she was a senior in high school, and had been sober for several years. *"The hardest thing is having him in the house. I can smell him and it gives me the shakes. My parents give him leniency, and it makes me mad. It is a whole new level of stress."*

Expectations, memories, regrets and dreams. Holidays are also especially impactful because events and feelings are being recorded, and recalled, using all of our senses. Typically holidays are celebrated with special food, music, activities, and gatherings so there are multiple sensory triggers. "Smell goes into the emotional parts of the brain and the memory parts, whereas words go into thinking parts of the brain…When you smell things you remember your emotions…it's very true," says Dr. Ken Heilman.[31] Just one more reason to guard who is invited to your celebrations, and to be sensitive to who is being drawn back into a hurtful past when you bring out the turkey, or hang the mistletoe next year.

Say, "Yes" to change

Concentrate on seeing the good things all around you, and focus on the needs of everyone in the family except the addict.

Whatever your family's dynamics have been it's time for you to set all the family hostages free, and to stand firm on your resolve to not let the alcoholic ruin one more family gathering. If you don't, you will eventually end up alone. Your other adult children will gravitate to their in-laws or other places of happiness and normalcy, taking their children with them.

Doing something radically different such as going on a trip can help transition from what was, or is, to what can be. Grief and gratitude can co-exist. Spend little time on grief (or anger if that's the stage you are in), and a lot of time being thankful. Change may feel strange at first, but if you like the new experiences, and can afford to repeat them, then they become your new traditions. If not, then going to The Grand Canyon, or swapping houses with another family in the same city or far away, will at least be a newer, happier memory. By next year, you'll probably feel more like revisiting the old traditions, or blending the old and new. *If you can't do something radically big, then go radically small.* Buy new Christmas ornaments, spend Thanksgiving helping at a homeless shelter, or let your sister-in-law host your grandson's birthday party at her house. When you are in emotional overload, simple is best. Cut out whatever you don't enjoy, strains your time, or wipes out your budget.

I like that the ornaments on mom and dad's tree are all ones that mom picked out the first year I came to live with her or ones that I made for her over the years. We also started our own tradition that first year of mom and I going to buy a new building for a holiday village that lights up and sits under the tree. It's grown so much that we now have a school, florist, bridge, people, bakery, pub and so much more...next year it will entirely circle the tree—or we'll have to start a second street. We're on the lookout for an outdoor skating rink. Someday, I'll be adding on to it and setting it up under Jessica's and my tree for our kids.

Unsupervised holiday visits

Do whatever you need to do, including spending a holiday by yourself or celebrating with the family another day, but don't allow the addict at family celebrations. *Visitation mandates are for access, not excess. Planning, shopping, paying for, and the outcome of holidays hosted by the parent for their children are not your responsibility.* The alcoholic needs to succeed, or fail, with their children on their own. Their kids need to know how different life with an addiction is versus sobriety because some-day they will have to make their own decisions. "For me just to see how those [friends'] families lived...what the rules and expectations were in their homes, had a huge impact because I was able to understand what I'd suspected, that a life like mine in childhood wasn't normal and it wasn't okay. And I started to get a much clearer picture of what I was aiming for."[32]

Your young charges may be disappointed, angry, embarrassed, or hurt if things don't go well with the using parent on their birth-day or other special occasion, but you can deal with their reac-tions when they return. Again, leave a buffer of transition time for them before they are rushed into extended family celebra-tions if you are going to do both on the same day. Give them privacy and time to talk with you about whatever is important to them before other family members arrive. Your job is to help them process and reflect. "I understand why you would feel that way," is really all they want to hear. "Can we talk more later about why I need to put the pocket knife your mom gave you away before your cousins get here?" or "I sense you are feeling rejected, we have a few minutes to talk now and lots more time tomorrow," are good ways to let them vent while leaving the door open for a deeper, stronger conversation later if needed.

Supervised holiday visits

The same rules and responses go for supervised visits on holi-days—no folding the addict back into the family mix just because it's easier, or you can't bear to think of them alone. Don't treat holidays different from other visits. *Everything needs to be on the user's dime during their private time celebration; if they want something special then they bring it, pay for it, and cleanup any mess.* Tell the parent they can show up at "X" time and need to be gone by "Y". If they've been using, they need to leave as soon as you realize what is happening. If you feel safer, or better able to limit the time together, meet at the movies, a local ski or sledding area, water park, faith gathering, or restaurant. If the user can't afford to do the primary activity offered at the meeting place, or it's too time consuming, suggest they buy their kids a hot chocolate, share a box of popcorn, or whatever works.

Help prepare kids in advance by talking about realistic expectations based on past experiences, "I know your mom promised she'd meet us, and your friends, at the mall for pictures with Santa on Christmas Eve morning, but maybe we should have a backup plan in case she shows up drunk." Or, "I get it, that you're still upset because dad forgot your birthday last year. What would you think about asking your brothers to go to the beach that week instead of waiting around here hoping dad remembers?"

Gifts

Both giving and receiving gifts can be difficult. Presents from addicted parents often reflect their disconnect from their children and reality. Their choices can be embarrassingly inappropriate, including items that are too childish, too adult, too expensive, grossly wrong sizes, or not what they promised. Many families talk about receiving gifts that were stolen, paid for with drug or crime-related money, or are worn and torn. *Let it happen.* Wrong sizes or age-inappropriate stuff can be exchanged, given away, or tucked into a closet for later. If you think a gift may be stolen check with police. Don't cover for the addict, or try to make it a teachable moment for kids by telling them, "She tried" or "he really does love you." Don't buy presents, and pretend their mom or dad bought them. Older sons and daughters will probably figure it out and, even if they don't, you are just hyping future expectations while prolonging the inevitable. You can't spend away hurt, or buy back trust.

Your kids/grandkids are continually being asked by friends, "What did you get? What did you do?" Even when not being asked, but just hearing how others answer those questions makes them feel bad about their own holidays. *"Everyone at school is excited about what they're going to get for Christmas. I just want my dad to come home off the streets, quit using drugs, and be with us – sober. This would be the best present ever. Secretly, I am a little jealous of things the kids at school have...the Xbox, iPhones, etc., but I feel guilty wanting them. I know we probably will never be able to afford those things."33*

If young ones want to give their parent a gift then suggest a drawing, book of poems, birdhouse, or baked treat. If they want to buy a gift, then tell them they can earn the money by doing a chore, or use some of their spending money. Let them pick out what they like and can afford, not what you like, or what you could afford. Keep in mind that addicts often return, sell, or pawn expensive gifts for booze or drugs. Money aside, it is devastating to their offspring when they find out. It's equally devastating if the user steals one of *their* presents, so also be cautious about what kids take with them, and what is lying around in sight at your place.

I always let Chad decide who he wanted to give 'holiday' school or scouting projects to when Brandy was around, even if it hurt my heart when he choose her over me. Kids need you to celebrate their efforts, and help them discover the joy of giving. **Don't tell your kids that it is a bad idea to give a gift to the addict, but try to see if they would rather give one to their sibling, best friend, or an aunt/uncle. Let them choose for themselves but guide them so that they think they made the decision entirely on their own.**
94

'You' stuff

We've talked about the emotions and needs of others in the family, but as usual, "and how are you doing?" seems to come almost as an after thought. Simply stated, you take care of yourself first because if you explode, the rest of the family will implode. So make a little "Me Time" list and check off something every day. Exercise, eat right, laugh out loud, engage in real and retail 'therapy', paint those toenails if you're a woman, or pound some nails or a punching bag if you're a man.

- **Dive into the pity pool.** It's okay to remember and grieve if you feel sad; to vent if you feel angry. Indulge in a little pity party, but don't make it a long one. It isn't healthy, and you don't have time. So look at old picture albums, watch family videos, or open the box of Mother's Day cards that you kept throughout the years. Cry and then move on.

- **Support.** When you're feeling overwhelmed call a friend, or family member, to help you through the tough time. Remember, however, that they will hold inside them whatever you have said long after you have set it aside. It can be hard for them to forgive the one you love/ loved for hurting you so deeply. Opening up to a counselor, or in a support group, is safer because the listeners are not emotionally invested. They will not repeat confidences to mutual acquaintances, and they will honestly tell you what they are thinking—some more directly than others.

- **"Keep your faith.** "Religion won't "fix" things, experts say. But it can help normalize them."[34] I think they are wrong. God has answered my prayers many times… things that weren't humanly possible came together. Regardless, spiritual belief helps put things in perspective and it gives you hope. "Belonging to a faith group means you have a community for support."[35]

95

- **Let a good memory, stay a good memory.** What has happened since your wedding, or your adult child's childhood shouldn't change good memories. Revel in the feeling of pride you had as your son walked across the stage and claimed his college diploma, the pleasure you felt when your wife leaned across the table to say, "I love you best", or the love displayed in, "Mommy's home, mommy's home," just before your daughter launched herself into your arms years ago.

- **Play 'remember when' with kids.** Young people need to see pictures and hear stories about their parents, and their childhood, regardless of their age. Laughingly recall, "Remember the Christmas your mommy (or whatever you call them, e.g. Brandy) bit Santa?" or "do you remember your dad (I'd say Donald to Chad) taking you to the pumpkin patch?" Good memories, favorite toys, pictures, or holiday memorabilia are lifelines to their past, and to their roots. Sharing them helps fill in gaps that time and separation create.

Holidays are about more than just making memories. They are also part of character and relationship building. Susi, the college grad, told me, "I have a very hard time with relationships. It's difficult to feel sympathy when someone is telling you their problems because compared to your own circumstances it doesn't even register on the chart. You are desensitized. My cousin Drew's father, like my mother, was into drugs and alcohol and we've talked a lot. He has the same issues that I do." The unwrapped gift of addict-free holidays is that young ones experience love, and learn healthy ways to express it to others.

One of the reasons why we have to deal with abuse is: It is contagious. It gets passed on from generation to generation.

Rick Warren

8
Words Matter: A Message for Parenting Grandparents

Talk the walk

No, it isn't a printing error. You also have to *walk your talk—but that follows.* Words define attitude, and in turn actions. Sometimes we need to start saying things that are not true before they can become true. It's decision time. From today forward, you can raise your grandkids, or you can parent. Either way, you'll be working hard and investing your heart, and either way, your adult child has failed as a parent (there I'm finally saying it...Brandy is a huge screw up as a parent) due to drugs and alcohol. The difference is *when you parent* you are choosing; when you *raise your grandkids* your addicted son or daughter chose for you.

In case you are not convinced.

No one can be both grandma and mom, or G pa and dad. Grandparents spoil their grandkids and send them home while they go back to work, read a book, or go golfing. Parents provide kids with food, home, clothes and a moral compass to guide them the rest of their life. They set boundaries and enforce consequences. They put their sons and daughters' needs above their wants. Both grandparents and parents can love, laugh, pray, and play equally well, but someone has to be in charge. Someone has to be there until childhood morphs into adulthood. *That person is parenting, and there is nothing 'second time around' about it.* The number of years between kids, your age, or whether they are your children by birth, adoption, or come to you out of need doesn't matter. *Genes make people, but hard work holds families together. We can, and will, talk about the definition of a family. First it's important to understand that your definition matters for your mental health, but it doesn't help the grandkids' unless they feel they belong, and feel that together you are putting down roots.*

At age six, Chad said, "God knows I'm at this place. I want to stay here in this place." He understood on a gut level that life away from alcoholism and drugs was good, and that God was watching out for him. It was important enough to Chad, for him to say it out loud. He trusted me enough to share his future, and his priorities. I didn't fully grasp the significance then, but I totally get it now.

What do grandkids hear?

They hear everything, and they internalize everything, because that's what kids do. Youth is self-absorbed. When *you* use skip generational or 'second time' terminology, *they* dig through their personal baggage and extrapolate, "I don't belong here, I'm different from all my friends, you are stuck with me, and you can't tell me what to do." As a defense mechanism, they jump immediately to, "You aren't my parent." And, they pull out the standard teen line early, and use it repeatedly, "You're too old to understand."

98

Don't reinforce these erroneous messages by using 'grand' as a prefix. Instead bolster their self-confidence by reinforcing their spot in your heart, and your immediate family. Simply say to everyone, "These are our twins, meet our youngest, or this is Ashton". At every opportunity use the words 'our family' and their name in the same sentence. "Our family is musical, and Britt sings at church", or "Finn thinks going someplace he and Shaquille can paddleboard would be fun. I agree and might even try it myself." **Inclusive words make you feel secure and loved, it reverses a little more of the damage done by your birth parents.**

Sign school, youth activities, and medical forms in the parent or guardian space and only define your legal relationship if doing otherwise is legally misleading, or makes you liable for financial obligations that are covered by government aid programs or continue to be the birthparent's responsibility.

What's in a name?

Parenting doesn't mean that your grandkids can't call you papa, nana, Grandma Peggy, mom, dad, Mimi, Grandmaman, or any other nickname. You just keep letting them know that they are family, and the name thing will follow naturally. *What they call you* is not important as long as it is a mutual decision between you and them, not their birth parents. Siblings may choose different names; older ones preferring grandpa or your first name, while a younger sister calls you dad. Let each kid know that you're okay with their choice, and their siblings' choices.

Bob and I dated seven years; he was *Mister Mom* for his two boys, while I was trying to bring stability and safety into Chad's world. We lived apart, but Bob was a huge part of our lives. I had permanent legal guardianship, but Chad still called me grandma; I still told everyone, "I was raising my grandson."

99

Bob asked me to marry him by typing the question into my computer while Chad sat on my lap. "Can I call you dad?" came out of Chad's mouth before I could respond. "I would be proud to have you for a son," responded Bob. Chad beamed; I had tears in my eyes. Later at a grocery checkout when Chad referred to Bob, with his gray hair, as "dad" and me, with my paid-for-highlights, as "grandma," it was hard on my ego, and we sure got startled looks. Back in the car, I told Chad whatever he called us was okay but it had to be a matched set, "Mimi and papa", "Grandma Joan and Grandpa Bobby," or "mommy and daddy." It was a hard decision for Chad because he wanted a dad desperately, but he also wanted to continue calling Brandy "mommy." Finally he settled on 'mom' for me, and 'mommy' for Brandy. After nearly eight years of referring to me as "grandma" he made the switch with only one slip.

A few years later, without discussion, Chad began calling "Brandy" by her first name and referred to her as, "my birth mom." I understood, and a part of me smiled, because he was sorting out his life and moving on. However, I also knew it had to be hard for Brandy. Years later, when he was in high school, she told me, "I still have problems with Chad calling me by my name. It cuts through like a knife, and is a wound that will never heal, no matter how many times I tell myself that it was my choices that make him feel, and do, what he does."

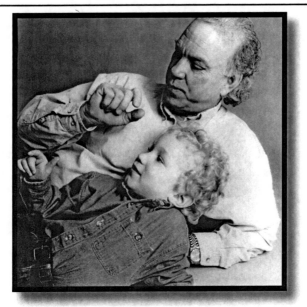

Bob, and Chad at age 3
Photo courtesy of Bob Zaikoski

Self-talk and depression

Brains are indiscriminate. It doesn't matter if yours hears you repeating the same words ninety times, or it hears ninety different people saying the same thing once. It's ninety impressions—so be very, very careful about your self-talk. Phrases like "second time around" and "raising grandkids" are constant reminders that you are older than many parents, and are in an entirely different situation from most of your friends. You *can make yourself feel old and depressed, not because of what you do—but because of what you say.* So when people ask you, "What are you up to these days?" reply, "Oh the usual, parenting, working, playing." You (and the kids) then hear a positive message that life is normal, balanced between family, earning a living, and having fun. The more you say it, the truer it becomes.

Negatively perceived messages pull you down both physically and emotionally. One study reported "94% of [custodial]

101

grandparents surveyed suffered from clinical depression"[36] The article went on to say that researchers are more apt to blame depression on the level of household income, lack of resources, and pre-existing conditions than the parenting role itself. However, they found that during times of transitioning the grandkids to the grandparent, or back to the biological parent, the added depression is significant.[37] I agree. Transitioning Chad to go live with his dad was the worst experience, and six months of my life. Humans don't do well with uncertainty and when we love deeply, having to let go is traumatic. Anticipating having to let go—while helping prepare the kids so they have the skills to get help if they need it, without alarming them, is God-awful. We can adjust our dreams when events force change; however, it takes awhile for our mind to convince our hearts that we are okay. Acceptance of a situation does not mean we approve, or like it, but acceptance creates a space where we can peacefully exist until our zest for living kicks back in.

I found that once Chad was back living with me, and I mentally jumped from being a 'grandparent raising' to 'parenting', I was more in control of my emotions, and more optimistic about the future. As I focused my energy, and found joy in being Chad's parent, I also found myself spending less time thinking about Brandy. I stopped comparing our family to other families, realizing that life is not trouble-free forever for anyone. At the time, my problems were just more out in the open than others.

Defining family

It's important to talk with grandkids, and help them decide how they want to describe their family to friends, adults, and when doing school assignments. Then when asked, "What does your daddy do?" or "write an essay explaining how the Afghanistan war affected your family," or "invite your grandma to Grandparent's Day," they know how to respond.

Explain that family can be whomever they want to include. It can be you and them, one birth parent and not the other, step or half siblings, or just them and the dog. Remind them of all the families they know that aren't the stereotype traditional family. "Traditional families" are now a minority in the majority of states.[38] Discuss how today's moms and dads are a mix of birth parents living together, single parents, stepparents, adopted parents, young parents, and older-by-choice parents. Chat about how some kids join a family by being born into it, others are adopted, live with their grandparents, are nieces or nephews, or just loved a lot--like foster kids.

"Family don't end with blood, boy." –Bobby Singer on Supernatural (TV)[39]

"Family isn't a blood relation, it is an unbreakable bond. Adoption is one of the best things that have ever happened to me."[40]

Whether you adopt your grandchildren, are their legal guardian, or just have custody—keep on letting them know that they are forever family. I always told Brandy, that she wasn't "born under my heart but in it." Same goes for Chad.

Just because a birthparent isn't always physically present, or the connection is random, doesn't mean their kids don't want to talk about them. Encourage all ages of children to keep sharing their feelings with you, even if it causes you to swallow your own hurt or anger, because that's how they will emotionally mature. *They need to know what they feel, before they can understand why they feel that way.* Chad once told his nana (my ex-husband's new wife) when he was very young and they were still active in his life, **"I hate my dad."** He was angry with her because, **"Nana said I can't hate my dad."** She was wrong, and I told him Nana was wrong. His counselor also told him Nana was wrong. Emotions are honest, and facts are facts. If a child's father abuses him, or his mother threw-up, do not deny it happened or that they don't have a right to be depressed, enraged, disgusted, or disengaged. Your job is to help him, or her, sort and process their feelings in appropriate ways. Denial is not healthy. The more you all can forgive (remember you can decide not to be bitter and forgive without forgetting) any wrongs, the faster happiness happens.

When Chad turned eleven he gave the following speech, which he wrote entirely himself, to inmates in the same 'seven-step-program' at the men's maximum security prison in Oregon where I ran into the problem years later with my turquoise shirt. "The best day of my life was the day my parents adopted me because my birth parents were mean to me and hurt me. Now I don't have to worry about ever going back to them because my grandma and Bobby adopted me. I'm glad I got adopted because now my dad takes me places and does stuff with me like dirt biking, and car shows. My dad and I, and my two older brothers, went dirt biking this weekend. I was faster than my dad was most of the time. We also built a corvette from scratch. My mom helps me when I need help. She helps me with my homework, and takes me places. She helps me when I'm sick, and takes me to church. In the future [sic], my birth dad helped me because he showed me what not to do when I have kids. My new dad shows me what to do when I have kids. I love my birth mom. She quit smoking and doesn't do drugs, and is a lot better than she was before. Her husband, Ryan, also quit drugs and now cooks for a homeless shelter. This is why being adopted was the best day of my life. The end.[41]

In a setting where macho means survival, inmates—two with tears in their eyes-- came up to him during a break and told him they liked his attitude and honesty. I couldn't have been prouder as my arm rested across Chad's shoulder, although they didn't know we belonged together. He was later given a plaque that was especially designed, and made, by the prisoners reading:

**For a Creative and Visionary Young Mind.
There is No Limit to the Things You May Achieve...
Or the Lives You Will Change Along Life's Journey.**

Know that you are changing lives. The ripple effect means the good you do now will long outlast you.

When you change, a whole new world finds you

A week before Chad moved back with me permanently, I retired from a thirty-year career in advertising. Instead of looking for a job in corporate America as planned, I started freelance writing so I could be there for Chad. *I lost a lot of social contacts, and even some friendships I treasured.* However, six years later Chad and I went on an all expense paid press trip designed to showcase family fun spots in Hawaii. I had twenty-five dollars in my pocket and a Visa and it was the trip of a lifetime. The editor at that time of *Portland Family Magazine, which I wrote two monthly columns and frequent feature articles for*, was Jennifer McCammon, who simply said to me, "I heard it in my heart to send you."

To keep Chad from the wrong crowd in high school, Bob and I took up skiing again in our sixties because Chad loved it and wanted to be on the high school ski team. I'm a better skier today, and enjoy it more now than in my twenties and thirties, because equipment is better, and I'm not afraid to say 'yes' to one challenge and 'no' to another. Bob's goal is to keep on skiing long past our eligibility for free ski passes for those over seventy. I joined a neighborhood bible study and have never laughed so much, or cried with so many women. Several of the friendships have extended to our partners. Life is good. I've mentally bumped back 'old age' into my late eighties or beyond...I just don't have time for it right now. Two weeks ago, I was asked to speak at a White House sponsored briefing about proposed changes in Foster Care regulations and budgets. My life isn't at all what I dreamed but better, in so many ways.

Get excited about the new paths opening up for you, even if you feel like right now you are headed over a cliff. I felt that way for years as, day in and day out, Chad was out-of-control and Brandy continued changing into someone I couldn't relate to. Again, I want to stress that you can't save everyone. I tried with Brandy, and then with Pepper, but I couldn't save either one. Do what you can, and for most of us that is to love out loud, cry silently, and take on new challenges everyday.

Just ask him how he did it, "he'll say pull up a seat
It'll only take a minute, to tell you everything."
Be a best friend; tell the truth, and over use I love you.
Go to work, do your best, don't outsmart your common sense.
Never let your prayin' knees get lazy
And love like crazy.
--"Love Like Crazy" by Lee Brice

 There's always a little truth behind every, 'just kidding';
A little curiosity behind every, 'just wondering';
A little knowledge behind every, 'I don't know'; and
A little emotion behind every, 'I don't care.'
Unknown

9

Counseling

Most disturbed teens, and younger children, let you know how they are feeling. They're in your face...yelling and defiant, or they're cutting, or they're preoccupied with blood and death. However, others aren't so open and consciously, or unconsciously, mask their feelings and behaviors. These adolescents may have nightmares, or wet the bed way longer than their friends, or spend a lot of alone time in their room. Some kiddos will hoard food, or they never cry, or they lie constantly but make the lies seem so plausible that you begin doubting yourself. Often troubled teens barter their bodies for affection trying to prove to themself that they are worthwhile, or because they want something in return. Others get sucked into the violence of gang life for similar reasons while searching for security and a pseudo 'family'.

"Anyone who has ever lived with addiction knows that the story may start with the addict but it rarely ends with the addict...no matter how you look at it, addiction is a family disease."[42] Trauma never stops, and it surrounds drug and drink abusers, taking a huge toll on everyone. Trauma stays in memory banks forever. We've mentioned trauma but haven't defined it, because we can't. It looks different in every family. Trauma can come from neglect, abuse, or rape. It can also be a result of kids worrying about their addicted parent, or having been a diaper-soaked-toddler wandering around looking for an empty baby bottle but instead finding syringes. It can be brought about if mom or dad is arrested, or from living on the streets. Children worry about parents who are running from the police, have disappeared, or are the local drug supplier. *Being separated from their parent is emotionally devastating for some, and a relief for others.* If children spend any time in foster care, of if they are separated from siblings, it's even harder.

Young ones exposed to trauma or continual stress, according to a wide body of research, have differently wired brains. It takes work to help them develop coping skills to handle situations, and personal interactions, that most people take for granted. Ironically kids who were abused consistently do better than kids who were abused inconsistently.[43] But none do well. "Alcoholic families tend to be chaotic and unpredictable. Rules that apply one day don't apply the next. Promises are neither kept nor remembered. Expectations vary from one day to the next...family members are usually expected to keep problems a secret...all of these factors leave children feeling insecure, frustrated, and angry."[44]

Group or private counseling is a safe place for you and the children to vent, and explore feelings, with the exception of the mandated reporter issues mentioned earlier. Your son, daughter or grandchild can talk about things they don't want you to know, or things they don't realize—without therapist intervention—that they are feeling. Counseling was a lifeline for both Chad and I, although sometimes he liked it and sometimes he resented going. Often teens will resist, but "just kidding, just wondering, whatever" taken to the extreme are calls for help regardless of what they say. If a family member has diabetes or a broken leg you wouldn't let their fear of what others think, or their distrust for a doctor, keep you from getting them medical help. Getting mental help is no different.

"The boys didn't want to go to counseling to talk about their alcoholic dad, so I tried to get them to talk," recalls Adriana. "They built up resentment, especially Kyle. He was less tolerant of Wes because he had been through a lot more. Wes used to cry and promise to be better, and the boys would believe him. Now I think back, or look at pictures with Wes sitting in a chair his head slumped over and I think, "That's what Kyle was seeing." You absolutely need to get professional help."

Today mental health care is more readily available through insurance than in the past. Community health clinics and private practitioners sometimes offer sliding fee options. Books, self-help videos, motivational speakers, information on the web, AA/Al-Anon or other guided support groups also can help. See the Resource Appendix at back of book for some other suggestions.

Getting healthy takes work

For years, after living with his birth dad, Chad could not sleep. He would try, and I would rub his back, literally for hours. Finally, when Chad was five, his counselor, working with his pediatrician, put him on nightly medication. It wasn't sleeping pills, rather a prescription to help his brain slow down. Even so, he would wake up multiple times during the night screaming, "Grandma," or "help". Officially diagnosed with Post Traumatic Stress Syndrome, it took years of talking, therapy, drawing pictures, dream catchers, music lessons (music is an outlet for emotions), and more talk before healing really happened.

I don't remember a smiling face, or a trip to the park. I don't remember wrestling, or watching TV. I don't remember anything that a dad and son should share. The thing is, that even when I think about him now, I don't have any anger towards Donald, but I also have no respect. The memories of beatings and waking to an alcohol-stench house haunt me in the worst of ways. When I was about ten or eleven I started having dreams that I couldn't find anyone in my house, except for a man standing outside the window. I would scream and run, but I couldn't find anyone. The dream went on and on.

Another dream I've had at multiple times throughout my life, is where I wake up in a room at the end of a hall, get out of bed, and go try to find my birth father. I find him; he's asleep, still drunk or hung over from the night before. I head into the kitchen, make myself a Pop Tart™, and turn on TV; it's Winnie the Pooh. I sit on the couch and start to cry. My birth father comes into the room, yells at me for watching TV and making my breakfast without him, and then pulls down my pants and spanks me with a metal spatula. Mom has told me this dream could be very, very close to reality.

The thing is that I don't regret what he did to me, I may not like it, but I am actually proud of overcoming it. It hurt me for years afterwards. But now that I am a man, God is saying, "Chad, this man hurt you, and you know what it's like. Now go help people."

That first dream that I was talking about had an ending. I couldn't find anyone, so I kept running, and eventually came to a long hallway filled with windows on both sides. I could see the man outside of them so I ran, and when I came to the end of the hallway I ran into the arms of my dad, Bob.

The first sessions with Chad's counselor, at age two, resulted in a lot of insight and suggestions for me based on his actions during therapy and elsewhere. Donald stopped taking him when they lived together, but I restarted Chad immediately after he was returned to my care. The older he got, the more the therapist directed suggestions to Chad as well as myself. Eventually, Chad went from weekly visits to intermittent, to dropping out altogether around third grade. When he was ten, Chad stopped taking the meds that helped him fall asleep. It was a decision he made after returning from scout camp where he had had to report nightly to the nurse's tent for his medication.

Chad's nightmares, by fifth grade, lessened considerably but he was still angry. He exploded in rage at times over seemingly odd things that always took a lot of follow-up conversation to get to 'the rest of the story'. The counselor, and I, tried to help Chad discover why he was so angry, and find ways to defuse it.

He still hated Donald, refused to even say his name. I knew Chad had to work through his 'dad mad' or be an emotional cripple because studies reveal that the ability to control one's emotions is more important than IQ when it comes to being successful in life. So the summer after fifth grade, I called Doctor Portland and it took just one session to get the breakthrough that had eluded us for years. She had Chad draw three columns on a white board, and label them, 'Brandy', 'Donald' and 'Chad.' Dr. Portland told Chad to list three things about Donald, that he did not like. No problem. A bad temper, mean, and hurtful were Chad's contributions. When she asked for good things, Chad said there were none. He resisted, but she persevered. After an extended silence Dr. Portland finally commented, "I recall he was pretty good looking." I threw in his carpenter skills, and Chad finally contributed that he was "a little fun." We did the same for Brandy.

Dr. Portland then explained that everyone is a box of puzzle pieces when born. The pieces that you choose, or reject, determine who you become. From the boarded items, Chad picked three of his parents' good traits, making comments like, "I'm pretty good looking too," and "I build neat things with Lego's." He then selected three things including "lies, bad temper, and argue" that he did not want to emulate. At the end, Dr. Portland pointed out that with some people there should be another column labeled "evil", and what Donald had done to Chad was evil. "Fathers," she said, "need to take care of, not hurt, their children." From that day on, Chad put his anger toward Donald pretty much to rest. This exercise won't work for every child but for Chad, who is very analytical and had worked through a number of issues already, it did. At the very least, a child can see through this exercise that they have choices, and control over their behavior.

1. Count to 10
2. take deep breaths
3. run around block (or walk)
4. walk away
5. try to be nicer
6. go to room
7. do push-ups
8. do jumping jacks
9. do sit-ups
10. go outside
11. play guitar
12. play baritone
13. watch TV while cool down
14. drink water
15. listen to music
16. draw
17. write
18. read
19. look at magazine
20. play a game by myself
21. lay down
22. sit + relax
23. don't argue
24. talk nicely
25. lift weights

25 Things I can do when angry to get nice again.

Chad, Age 10

Addicts and alcoholics are always 'using' or 'recovering' but never 'recovered' as in permanently, and forever, sober. So you are protecting their kids by giving the young ones time and space to grow from helpless, hurt children into emotionally strong adults who can deal with relapses, and other bumps, when necessary. In the critical years that they live with you, help them acquire the life skills necessary to temper their emotions with logic. Teach them to separate from their past, and to set crucial boundaries--now if there is contact, and in the future if they choose to continue, or reconnect, with their birth mom or dad.

Broken promises break kids

In high school, when Chad became suicidal, it was because of Brandy, but I didn't know that until it came out during counseling. My relationship with Brandy, when I started high school, was very good. I would tell her anything and she would tell me anything too. She was pretty much my best friend, and I loved her a lot. But then things started to happen. She started to not call me as much, and I talked to mom about it. Then she stopped calling altogether and wouldn't answer my calls. She "lost her job." I was scared and started to get depressed. I pretty much thought that I had lost my best friend. I couldn't cope and started writing poems about death, and contemplating suicide. But I couldn't do it because I thought that she would still come back and there would be a very good explanation for it all.

The answers weren't what I wanted. She may have not broken her promise about doing drugs again, but she might as well have. She was drinking a lot, pretty much an alcoholic. I couldn't cope at all. Suicide seemed pretty good. But I didn't want to die. I just wanted to take away the pain. So I started cutting myself. And it lasted almost a year and a half.

One night a parent of one of Chad's friends rang our door at midnight saying Chad was on the phone with their son, and he was saying that he was going to kill himself. We needed help.

114

I called everyone I knew the next day looking for a male therapist experienced in working with high school boys having anger and abandonment issues. We needed someone Chad could relate to, and who could relate to him. *Brandy and Donald caused the problems, but Chad had to own and work through them.*

I lost sight of God completely. I didn't even want to think about God, until I had somebody tell me that I was just being stupid. When they said that I had gone too far and that I needed God to get out, I believed them. So I repented, and I made the decision that I would live a life of happiness. I decided not be brought down by my past, but to use it to my advantage. I told Brandy to stay out of my life, and that I didn't want to talk to her ever again. That was a conversation that repeated itself again years later—for the last time. I'm done.

"Counseling was very beneficial," says Bob. "It gave me insights on what I was doing wrong, and what bothered Chad, but he was afraid to say. It let me say things I was afraid to share with him. It helped bring out, and then bury, animosity because it helped us understand what he was going through, and how his mind was working. We worried that nothing we tried before was reaching him."

I learned to let Chad cool off, and not to talk things to death. Bob learned to never, regardless of the provocation, threaten violence but that he had to take a much firmer stand, and not leave all the disciplining to me. Chad learned to suggest alternatives when he disagreed with a guideline or mandate, and appropriate ways to express feelings when the answer was still "no". We all learned again that anger not only masks fear or pain but also sadness, frustration, or embarrassment.

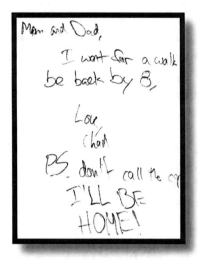

Mom and Dad,

I wont for a walk
be back by 8,

Lou
Chad

PS. don't call the cp
I'LL BE
HOME!

Chad, high school

Was there also normal 'teen stuff' going on also? Absolutely, and the counselor helped Bob, and I, separate the issues. He gave us information and hope. He helped guide us through issues we had no experience in confronting.

Chad's counselor also showed us what we needed to change with our parenting and communication styles. Chad used profanity and anger as hostage takers. He saw everything as his 'right' and nothing as a 'privilege' or 'responsibility'. Painful as it was, there were times when I had to call his bluff and say, "I will call the police because you are out of control. I don't want you to have to go to a foster home, but if you walk out that door then that is what I have to do to keep you safe." I never did, but I started dialing a fake number once or twice. I probably would have followed through because the alternatives weren't good. It shredded my heart, but it was my last resort. When our relationship grew less intense, Chad explained how hurt and scared he was when I did this because he had been in foster care as a toddler. I apologized and we talked it out. **It's hard to even remember being that angry all the time. I do not know what I would have done if I were mom, I just remember it scared me.**

On Empoweringparents.com, I later found similar advice from Debbie Pincus, a Licensed Mental Health Counselor, *"You may need to say to your child, 'If I'm feeling endangered here, I will need to call the police. I don't want to do it, but I may have to.'"* Don't accept behaviors from family that you wouldn't tolerate from a stranger or casual acquaintance; you deserve respect and to feel safe in your own home. An act of violence is an act of violence. James Lehman, MSW, lived a rough life and understood that with many kids a stern look, lecture, or normal conversation and consequences do not work. *He constantly advised parents to act, not react, and to tell children with anger and violence issues 'this is our house and we are in control; upset us and bad things are going to happen.'* *"Kids,"* he said, *"get a sense of power from acting out and they use that power to solve the problem instead of learning how to cope with life. These children don't learn the mechanics of problem solving or how to deal with their feelings appropriately. And that's an important and critical misstep, because it leaves them on one side of the cliff with no bridge to the next phase of life, the phase where they learn to negotiate, to get along with others, and to solve the problems that arise without losing control."*[45]

Drugs change people

Brandy took Chad's half-sisters to AA meetings so they "Could see the healing, the solution," she said. I strongly disagreed with her thinking. Going to the meetings was all about Brandy showing off her daughters, and about her own healing. My granddaughters' innocence was long gone, but if Brandy had wanted the girls to heal and to learn coping and relationship skills she would have been taking them Al-anon, the AA sister organization, that specializes in informing and supporting family members. During this same time frame, my oldest granddaughter, Pepper, was also seeing a school counselor twice a week at the time, "It's a safe place to go and talk," Brandy mused. "Things may still come back to bite us in the butt, but at least they have always been in a loving environment...not a foster home." **Brandy has a warped sense of 'loving environment' given all that happened; but that aside, it's a bad idea talking to school counselors. If kids are having that big a problem then they should see a private practice counselor. Personal life and school life need to be separate.** Chapter thirteen, *Parenting a Child with Special Needs & Challenging Behaviors*, explains why we feel this way.

Adolescents being raised by alcoholics or drug users have no experience in healthy parent/child relationships. A lot of addicts try to be their children's friend, and tell them what they want to hear, not what they need to hear. As kids get older they begin seeking advice from peers because separating from parents is their job. When mom/dad becomes a friend their son or daughter listens, and responds, as if they were a true peer. That should scare you down to your socks. You, the sober parent or grandparent, must be the authority figure defining expectations and rules for kids, and also for the addict if they are still in your lives. You have to enforce limits when necessary. Some users are mean, and mentally or physically abusive—offering no relationship. Most tend to be erratic—so their kids never know what to expect. Again, you have to be the one who is unchangeable (stable not inflexible), in control, and responsible. You have to be the grownup.

Death

When death is involved, grief counseling and/or support groups can be especially helpful. The world-renown Dougy Center in Portland, Oregon works with youth and their adult caregivers in peer-focused support groups using "talking circle" time, and a variety of indoor and outdoor play activities. Children, teens, and young adults are grouped together by age, type of death, and connection to person who died. On their website, a client quote reads, *""Expect the unexpected. Emily actually danced and sang after I told her that her mother died. I was shocked. Later I realized the relief we both felt. The relationship had been filled with her [mom's] alcoholism, lies and illness." father of Emily."*[46]

"Grief never ends, but it does change in character and intensity. Many grievers have compared their grieving to the constantly shifting tides of the ocean; ranging from calm, low tides to raging high tides that change with the seasons and the years."[47]

Tips for working with children who have experienced death of a parent can be found at the Dougy website www.dougy.org.

"Every time we drive by the cemetery Charlie says, "Hi Daddy,"" says Patty whose partner died several years ago. "When Rick[48] first started asking me out I refused to date him because he was an alcoholic, and after dealing with my brother, Mike, I wasn't going to get involved. Rick chose to cut back a lot, and basically only drank on special occasions. He went out one night with friends that he used to get unbelievably drunk with, and slipped into his old ways. Not only did he pay a price, but also Charlie and I continue to pay a price every day. Every time Charlie accomplishes something, or asks to learn how to do something new that normally a father figure

would teach him, or when he asks questions about his dad, my heart breaks a little. One small decision can predetermine not only your life but also the lives of those you care about. Charlie will only ever know his dad as a marker on the ground, and the stories he hears, but he'll never really know him."

When kids become adults

Our story with Brandy and Pepper doesn't have a happily ever-after ending. Their final exit last year wasn't kind, or pretty. I feel nothing anymore—not even sadness except for all of Brandy's children. Brandy is finally, forever and always, out of Chad's and my lives. This time I won't be reaching out, or giving in. After twenty plus years I have finally made peace with myself. I don't like Brandy as a person, or as a mother. We all have the choice to accept someone as they are, try to change them, or let them go. My current screen saver is Josh Jameson's saying, "There comes a time when you have to choose between turning the page and closing the book". Counseling helped me be able to finally close the book.

You would think that an addict/alcoholic could at least be thankful for the help that someone tried to give them. My mom and I thought that Brandy would feel that way, and we were completely wrong. She didn't only ruin her own life, but cared more for the people she was hurting, like her kids (not me though), than the people who were trying to help her. When I finally "closed the book" it was extremely hard, but it had to be done. I wouldn't let my mom put in any more love and time into someone that didn't even care anymore. It wasn't worth the pain to anyone, anymore.

Faith connection

Everyone has his, or her, own spiritual beliefs and we aren't trying to change yours. Jesus is our savior but we respect your choice. Faith is absolutely a gift you give yourself, and your children. When something isn't humanly possible we all need the hope, and help, that only a higher power provides. I wouldn't have made it without God. He brought friends into my life that prayed for me, and cried with me, and held Chad's toes to the fire.

The biggest thing for me to remember is to have faith in God during the good times as well as the bad times. Sometimes we forget that when things are going well it's because God is the one that is doing things in our life. We need to thank him and remember that if it were not for God, our lives would not have purpose.

 That's all drugs and alcohol do,
they cut off your emotions in the end.

Ringo Starr

10
Emotions Don't Need a Label...
Or Do They?

"Some days it's in my head. Some days it's in my heart," said a friend of mine. Fair enough, so let's talk about getting your head and heart in a safe place. You have the ability to think, feel, evaluate, and act. With family it's easy for emotion to override the other functionalities; however, for your own peace try to consider facts and feelings independent of relationship. You probably wouldn't be friends with people doing the things that your addicted loved one does on drugs. You can excuse, or tolerate, one or five or a dozen things that offend your soul, but you can't live that life forever. The inner conflict will steal your happiness, and stress will destroy your body.

"Focus on what you want, not what you didn't want to happen to you. Focus on your goals," said Rick Warren in an on-line newsletter. If you have trouble letting go of the addict, or in

setting boundaries, and harbor unrealistic expectations check out www.addictsmom.com. There is a lot of wisdom and support shared in their chat rooms, blogs, and other resources. "It gave me such comfort to…be able to put something out there online at any time during the day and have twenty people respond back with, 'Hey, we know. We've been where you're at. We feel for you. We're praying for you,'" said Brenda Sherwood of Ohio whose son died of a heroin overdose."[49] I do not know how many of the 20,000 members are single parents, or raising grandchildren, but many have other kids, and each knows the pain addictions create.

What's the worst thing that can happen if I let go of the addict?

Nothing different than if you do not let them go. They can over-dose, kill someone when high, commit suicide, or die of complications from their addiction. My sister-in-law, Sandi Dingle, has been there for her son Mike, who is now in his late twenties and struggled for years with alcoholism and depression. Mike has no children or wife, but his problems have landed him in and out of jail, and his actions have hurt his siblings.

"At some point," Sandi says, "you have to ask yourself, 'Am I helping, or enabling?' Asking your child to move out is SO hard. The first time I gave Mike the boot I did not know where he was for over two months. It was winter in Minnesota and all he had was the clothes on his back and a light jacket. It was still the best thing I ever did for him. He finally got a job and began to 'figure it out'. Meanwhile, I lost a lot of sleep, cried a ton of tears, and prayed I was doing the right thing." When I asked her, "How do you deal with the constant concern he'll attempt suicide again?" Sandi shared, "This is probably the most difficult part for me. I've done all I can, offered counseling, taken him to Narcotics Anonymous (NA) and AA meetings, even called the police when I thought he was a danger to himself or others, which got him a four-day stay in the hospital. But I know that in the end, if he does kill himself, I did all I knew to do and that helps give me peace. Praying helps too. You do what you can, and give the rest up to God."

After you face the worst that can happen to the addict, make a list of the worst that can happen to their children, their siblings, and you if you stay connected.

If you do not kick an addicted adult child out, then everyone in the family is at risk. "If drugs were found in your home, you could be arrested, you could lose your job, your other children, your home."[50]

The addict or alcoholic could get their kids hooked and suicide may be their way, not their addicted parent's way, out. You shouldn't have to think about these things, but you do. Total separation is crucial, but we know that your heart takes a forever hit. Thomas Taylor's daughter is anorexic and, in many ways, it's similar to a drug or alcohol addiction. A few years ago Tom, and his daughter Kathryn's doctor, held an intervention; Kat (23-years-old, 78 pounds and 5'8") would have been dead within two weeks without it. At first she refused treatment, but threatened with a 72-hour lockdown in a psychiatric ward, she capitulated. She told her dad, "I know you're doing this because you love me, but right now, I hate you." "Okay," he replied, "I can live with that." What he couldn't live with was her decision 24-hours later to leave the hospital and he told her, "Kat, I've spent all the love, time, effort and money on you that I can give. If you go home, I'm done. I'm finished. I'm walking away. You can take me to the airport, I'll hop on a plane, and I know that I will likely never see you again. But I am going to be crystal clear on this: if the City of San Jose calls me to claim your body, I won't do it. I won't come back down here. I will let them deal with you the way they do for any unclaimed dead vagrant. I won't be there for you in death if you die by suicide."

Tom explained, "We'd reached rock bottom. The bottom line is, Dad can't fix it. Dad is used to fixing everything, but in the case of addiction, it's something Dad can't fix. I sat by her

124

bedside and texted her godmother, "I'm finished and heading back home. Kat won't go into treatment. The doctors give her a 30% chance of survival, and I'm not backing her on this decision. I won't be a part of her life anymore." I meant EVERY WORD. Kat's decision was the embodiment of selfishness. "Hey! Look at me! Watch me die slowly, right in front of your eyes! I choose this!" After a few minutes, Kat relented in tears." A month later she made it back to work at 80% of normal body weight. Her mother, his ex-wife, also has an eating disorder and they both had to release her from their lives. You hope letting go helps the addict bounce back, but you can't hold yourself responsible if they don't.

Untangling fact from emotion

As a kid, I thought, "How could I not feel the way I do?" The answer, I now think, is that I didn't understand how to feel. If I were put in a foster home today, I would not want my family visiting me. Seeing the people that you love most, but can't be with, hurts. It hurts to sadness. It hurts to think. It hurts to question. How do you think I ("f" word) felt? Words can't describe the feeling. Nothing can. But it's a feeling of hopelessness, of wondering. Feeling like you need something, like you're starving, but can't get food. Like your purpose in the world is lost. I think sometimes, "I probably should've died when they hit me," or "they never even loved me."[51]

Today, I understand that it isn't a matter of needing to know "how to feel" but rather just acknowledging how you actually do feel—owning it—so you can move on, that's important.

"Sixteen thousand—that's how many words we speak, on average, each day. So imagine how many unspoken ones course through our minds. Most of them are not facts but evaluations and judgments entwined with emotions—some positive and helpful...others negative and less so."[52] In other words, our brain is constantly bombarding us with thoughts. It takes a fact such as, "My son, Robert, stole from our neighbors," and adds, or subtracts, from it as you grapple with the implications. The fact morphs into, "My son is bad. I was a terrible dad. Robert is going to prison; his life is over. My neighbors will talk and how will my grandkids feel?" Or, "There must be a mistake, Robert wouldn't steal." The reality is that the event (burglary by your son) is the only fact. The rest is judgment, projection, and emotion.

If you stop and consciously say, "*I am having the thought* that Robert stole and stealing is bad." Then you can analyze what emotions that thought triggers in you. It may be: "I *feel afraid* that Robert will steal from other friends. I *feel embarrassed* because he was arrested, and it's on the news. I *feel ashamed* of Robert. *I feel angry* that Robert's actions hurt his kids. *I feel that I can trust* Robert, there must be a mistake."

Once I started identifying what emotions I was experiencing when something involving Brandy happened, including feeling embarrassed, scared, angry, hurt, confused, bewildered, weak, obligated, abandoned, powerless, numb, depressed, helpless, hopeful, happy, peaceful, and grateful, I was able to separate her actions from my conjecture and baggage. I realized that I was filtering most things through what I thought a mom 'should do' or 'ought to feel' instead of considering what I wanted, and personally felt.

The process of labeling facts, judgments, or emotions allows you to "... expand your choices. You can decide to act in ways that align with your values."[53] Thoughts and emotions are a kaleidoscope of change, but values usually don't vary. Mentally, or on paper, list options. Continuing with the Robert example, possibilities could include apologizing to neighbors, explaining your fears to them, avoiding them, or asking for their help. Then verbalize your feelings, "I'm so sorry that Robert would steal from you. Robert is an addict and we don't

126

let him come over anymore." Or, "I am embarrassed, and I don't know what to say. I would really like to pay for new locks for your home and garage. It won't replace what was stolen, including your trust in Robert, but it would make me feel better." Another possibility is, "Please press charges, then maybe Robert will get the help he needs in jail. Nothing we have tried has worked."

It's only when your thoughts, emotions, values, words, and actions are in sync that you will be free. Start with as large steps as you can manage when changing, or cutting off, your relationship. Write a letter. Refuse collect calls from jail. Agree to meet only at a counselor's office, or tell the user that you don't want to hear from them again.

Love lasts

Past love can last by holding onto good memories. Future feelings aren't so predictable. About five years into the mess of Brandy's having babies-out-of-wedlock, welfare, embezzlement, drugs, court appearances, counseling, physical abuse, finances, and dealing with child services, I realized I was depressed. A startling and freeing moment came when Chad's counselor asked me, "Do you love your daughter?" I replied with the only thought I could wrap my mind around, "Well, I do not like what she is doing." "No," asked Dr. Portland, "Do you love her? It is okay not to you know. We do not have to love our children."

Paradigm shift. Embraced it in my head, but it took me years to accept it in my heart. If eventually walking away from Brandy makes me a bad mom, or bad person, in someone else's mind, too bad. It's their problem, not mine. Friends, who gave Brandy a baby shower after I said it would enable her to continue not working and to stay in an environment where drugs were being used, criticized me. I was again criticized when I filed for custody of Chad. The criticisms stopped over the years, and oddly the people criticizing me drifted away. I will always love Brandy, the little girl; but as I've written before, the woman she chose to become, I don't want around. She is like a chameleon, telling whoever she is with what she thinks they want to hear. You don't have to decide if you love, hate, like, or think your child or spouse will ever recover right now. You just have to shift your focus off of them and onto yourself, their kids, and the rest of your family.

I want to leave you with the word 'hope'. Cling to it...even when it's as tenuous as a single lit match that you are sheltering during a hurricane. *"If you lose hope, somehow you lose the vitality that keeps life moving, you lose that courage to be, that quality that helps you go on in spite of it all. And so today I still have a dream," said* Martin Luther King Jr. in one of his speeches. His dream cost him his life, but his kids live in a not perfect, but better, America because of his courage. What you are doing everyday is Medal of Honor courageous because you are changing not only your life, but also the life of future generations.

A heart memory: **Our mother and son dance at my wedding.**

128

All violence begins with disconnection.
All outward violence begins as inner loneliness.

Glennon Doyle Melton, Author

11
Difficult Questions, Powerful Answers

Children of alcoholics or addicts will always *have* questions, and will *always be asked* questions. Their questions of us deserve answers. Other people's questions to them deserve acknowledgment--not details--regardless if asked by a neighbor, teacher, schoolmate, great-aunt, doctor, or strangers at a checkout counter.

The most difficult question I was ever asked was, "How do I feel about my birth dad?" and it is a question I have never been able to answer. The feelings that I do have for him are so mixed and jumbled up. I may never know truly how I feel, but I'll take the future memories.

There is no simple answer when you are confronted with, "Why did dad hit you?" or "Why can't my sister live with us, grandma?" Just as there are multiple possible responses when children are asked, "Why do you live with your grandma, is that drunk really your mother, or why haven't you finished drawing a picture of your family?"

"Why do these [type of] questions trouble us? Because we know instinctively—and our children feel it deeply—that people ask personal questions only in situations they perceive as abnormal..."[54] All you can do is prepare yourself, and your kids, for the moments in life when you define your future by accepting and moving beyond the past. "If a kid doesn't have the correct information about why mom or dad is dealing with this problem of addiction, they will make up their own reasons...and often these ideas or stories will get played out in adulthood," according to Tonya Meeks, a licensed therapist.[55]

Be there for the lightweight everyday stuff with kids, and they will come to you with the heavy things. *Addicts destroy their children's willingness to trust so you have to start in the hole they dug.* Acknowledge that their parent isn't reliable, but that you are. Keep their confidences, answer questions honestly, and be consistent.

To a certain degree questions have to be answered truthfully, and to a certain degree they don't. Some questions shouldn't be answered at all. For example, when I was really little and asked, "Why is mom in jail?" The truth would have hurt me more than a non-specific comment. Knowing the impact of the truth and being forthright, while framing your response, is what responsible parenting is all about.

Questions are doors to walk through

Children's questions can catch you off guard with their content or timing. When they do surprise you, let them lead the conversation at least until you know where you're headed! Listen to their words, and watch their body language. Often what they verbalize isn't the real issue. Adolescents are notorious for masking concerns, questions, and insecurities with seemingly indifference or sarcasm such as, "Whatever. Dad's a douche.

I'll run away before I go to a foster home again." Or, "How much are they paying you to take care of me?" What they are really saying is, "I'm scared. Dad embarrasses me. I do not want to get hurt again." Be truthful, but age-sensitive. Leave some things on the 'did not ask', 'did not tell' list. Double-check your assumptions by paraphrasing or asking an open-ended questions such as, "How does that make you feel? Or, "what makes you ask if your mom is a dealer?'"

When hard-hitting questions or emotionally loaded comments are thrown at you in public, or you need time to think, agree to talk later. To keep from losing the moment, or increasing your youngster's stress level, explain that they deserve a better answer than the place, or time constraints, allow. Make a time commitment for later in the day if possible; too much time and they will think you are covering up something, or brushing them off. Sometimes, I shared what I knew immediately. Other times I needed to talk to counselors about options, or try to gather/confirm what I thought I knew before responding to Chad.

A reader's comment in an "Ask Amy" column, "You mentioned that long drives are a good way to talk to kids. My mother was famous for this! Whenever she had a serious topic to discuss she would wait until she was transporting me to one activity or another... my teenage self hated it, but my grown-up self loves her for it,"[56] caught my eye because I did the same thing. I also discovered that play really does stimulate confidences. "I felt a little guilty sneaking off [skiing] but by afternoon, as the words tumbled out of Daniel's heart that had not been shared in the hustle and bustle of home, I felt great joy and gratitude to be there," said Mary, a Washington mom. Don't bring up sensitive matters, or try to answer questions with complex or troubling answers during dinner, before school, while they are doing their homework, or watching a favorite TV show. Answering hard questions can require extended conversation so timing is important. But don't go on and on unless they continue asking questions and making comments.

Helping develop self-confidence and good communication skills in young people

Any time a conversation is initiated by your child or grandchild, find out what prompted it. Curiosity? Comments from others? A video shown at school? Or maybe something they stumbled on in a drawer at home, or on social media? Their response will help you decide what information to share (or withhold based on their age and their need to know), and how to frame your response. You'll also discover if they need some coaching, or help in handling a social or school situation. Anticipate circumstances and questions they will face, and discuss facts and communication skills with them before they are needed.

There are no right or wrong answers when questions or circumstances are personal, but children caught off-guard by emotionally charged remarks, or touchy family-related school assignments, frequently strikeout verbally or physically. Or, they withdraw into themselves. By being prepared, they can handle most situations. *In your discussions include tips on how to request help, avoid giving out inappropriate personal information, and defuse uncomfortable situations. They don't want to offend adults who do have authority over them, or set themselves up for ridicule from peers.* Knowing what to say, as well as knowing about voice tone and body language can make a huge difference. These life skills will eventually put them ahead of the curve in getting and keeping jobs, maintaining relationships, and feeling good about themself.

I explained to Chad before kindergarten, and reminded him often during those early years, that he could always ask teachers, scout leaders, or whomever he was with to call me if he felt overwhelmed. Today, he doesn't remember our conversations, but back when he was so angry and scared that he would barely hold it together at school, I know it helped. We had lots of screaming and crying at our house during Chad's elementary years. In junior high and high school Chad punched holes in

132

walls, threw things, or swore, but never once did he use the 'free pass' or get into trouble outside our home.

"Children are often the silent victims of drug abuse"[57]

At some point kids realize that their parent's arrests and inappropriate behaviors, such as being stoned and walking down the street with a knife, are noticed or make the local news. If something does happen, it's better they hear from you that it's on TV or in the local paper than from a schoolmate, teacher, or other adult. Sadly, some people gossip, others distort the truth. Best that your children know the facts and how to verbally distance themself from their parent's actions. Emphasize that they have no obligation to correct, verify, or add to anyone's knowledge. Teach them that responding respectfully, but saying only what they want others to know, will eventually stop most people. Conversely, responding inappropriately to insensitive questions or thoughtless comments will peak, and prolong, unwanted attention. Make up questions, and practice possible responses with them. Following are some things to consider, followed by questions and responses that you can easily modify to meet your situation.

Prepare

- Anticipate stressful situations and questions.

- Explore with your child how *they feel, and what information they would like to share.* Help them set boundaries because children of addicts often have none. Remind them to never post, tweet or snapshot in anger or without carefully thinking about, "Do I want the world to know this and will I feel the same way five years from now if it comes up in a job interview?"

133

- Suggest *key phrases* for responses. "My mom can't take care of me right now," or "My dad said you can call him if you have questions. Do you want his cell number?"

- *Role-play.* Do it often. Keep it brief. Make it fun (like role reversals where they get to be you or the adult, and you play their part).

- Reinforce their right not to give information that makes them uncomfortable, even if the questioner keeps asking the same thing in different words. Help them respectfully give the same response as many times as necessary. Media trained personnel for corporations and government do this all the time. Practice exit-strategies such as physically walking away or saying, "excuse me" and changing subjects.

- *You* should give only answers to others that you would *want the kids* to hear whether talking to family, friends, or strangers. *Always assume what you say will be taken out of context and passed along.*

Defusing Phrases

- *Thanks for being concerned,* but I don't want to talk about it.

- *Good question, wish there was an easy answer.*

- *It would mean a lot to me* if you would stop asking.

Deflecting Phrases

- I live with Grandpa Z. just like you (or a mutual friend) live with just your mom/dad/aunt/foster or step-mom.

- Yeah it is embarrassing, but I try to ignore him when he's drinking and I hope you will too.

- Families are different. Have you seen (give TV show that is currently on with a similar or untraditional family mix)?

- My grandparents adopted me (may want to add "ask them" or "the judge said").

Debrief

- Ask open-ended questions about how they felt during the conversation, and now.

- Compliment effort.

- Consider alternative reactions and refine answers to help them feel in control rather than defensive, apologetic, or experiencing guilt or anger.

- If the situation seems volatile ask if they would like you to step in. If it is a matter of safety you need to intervene regardless, but tell them what you will say, do and why. For example, "You handled that well; however, since James threatened you with a gun I have to tell the principal, police, and his parents for everyone's safety."

- Practice. Practice. Practice.

Examples that can be easily modified depending on your situation, and the child's age.

Why do you live with your grandma and grandpa? Because they love me, just like Jamal's dad and step-mom love him. Do you want to get started on our science project?

Your mom's a drug addict/seller (or sexually derogative description, etc.). I'm not my mom.

Heard your old man's in prison (or it must break your heart to see your son in jail)? Thanks for understanding that it is too personal and/or hard to talk about.

Why is your mom so old? Why is your mom blond, Irish, short/tall? We are all different. (Discuss hurtful "labels" and why they should never be part of their response).

You can't hate your father. You don't know my dad or why I feel like I do. I respect your feelings; please respect mine. Or, "My counselor says it is okay because my dad was mean to me."

I am sorry about your father. Thank you.

Your son/daughter is so cute, or you do not look like your mom (and you are not the parent). Thanks, I think he/she is special. Or shrug and smile, *there is no need to correct statements unless you choose to do so.*

Your dad won't notice if you take a couple of beers, he's drunk all the time anyway. You're wrong, he'd notice and I'm not stupid enough to drink and lose my license.

My mom says your dad abandoned (beat, raped, etc.) you. It makes me feel sad/bad/mad when people talk about my family. (Diverting tactic: We had better hurry, the bell is about to ring. Defusing: Then tell her she needs to talk to my aunt.)

Mom asked me to score her some marijuana. How did that make your feel? Then based on response, "I'm proud you told her no," or "thanks for telling me. Do you want me to call her?" If they said no, *and they are old enough (otherwise you do have to call and report it to their caseworker and police),* then suggest they respond by calling her and/or telling her next time, "Mom, don't ask me again. I won't ever do it—even if it was legal, I wouldn't because you can't handle it."

 Memories take us back.

Dreams take us forward.

Kushandwizdom

Perception is reality, so deal with it

When he was three, after living with Donald for eight months, Chad asked me, "Remember when I was good enough and you came and got me?" Heartbreaking question, simple answer, but it took years for my words to replace his distorted reality.

Kids will not hear, or accept, your answers if you do not address their emotions, as well as, their request for facts. Don't over react to delivery unless they are being verbally abusive or offensive. Calmly clarify what you think they are asking and let them know you will answer them if they show you respect. For example, "Grace, I think you are saying that you are afraid your dad will come back and that you will be forced to live with him. He may return, but the judge says you'll live with me until you graduate, or longer if that's your choice. We can talk about it more now, or take a ten minute break, or drop it, but I won't talk to you when you are screaming or swearing at me."

137

Be empathic; no lecturing. Your kids will make up their own mind regarding their parent's actions—you can't force them to think or feel like you do, so make your point and drop it. There are words, phrases, and actions that ignite most people so try to make factual (or 'I' rather than inflammatory 'you') statements. Explain why you are bringing up something that could be hurtful or seemingly out-of-the blue to them. For example, "Jerome, remember when you asked me a few months ago if I knew where your mom is? Well, I just heard…" or "Summer, I overheard some of your friends talking in the stands at the game yesterday about your dad and…"

Talk to your kids or grandkids, but know that sometimes you have to live with the fact that they will not respond. Just be there when they are ready.

Surround your kids with good role models

During his first four years in elementary school Chad struggled with his Post Traumatic Stress, so I requested nurturing, female teachers. After that, because of Bob's and my ages and because Chad needed healthy young men in his life, I looked for young, male teachers and coaches that showed common sense, structure, and playfulness. We picked a high-energy church with a large, active youth ministry where the pastors and the small male group leaders were mature in their faith, but had a sense of humor. From ski coaches to family and friends, we were blessed with the best-of-the-best role models—of varying ages, sex and backgrounds--in Chad's life.

A number of people greatly influenced me; some were constants in my life and others were there for a little while. It's important at first to help your kids find good people, but then you have to let go and let God bring who He wants them to be around. Even one comment can change you forever.

I can't begin to list everyone who has helped me become who I am today but Carol, Randy, Ryan and Allie Walch are, and always will be, my second loving family. Dr. Chris (Christine Portland), my first counselor, went to the edges of the earth to help me. Jack Walker, my high school ski coach, pushed me to my physical limits and JB, another of my ski coaches, helped change my mental state, how I thought about life and felt about myself. Skiing turned my life around. Chris Nye preached the word of God in a way that I could understand and relate to. Jessica, my wife, showed me that there were more people that I could trust and love in the world than just my families. Yeah, teaching your kids is one thing, but ultimately they are going to learn from those they surround themselves with. At that point, it's just about prayer.

Help children define themselves without assuming misplaced responsibility, or guilt, for their addicted parent's actions. It is not a one-time conversation, but takes continual dialogue with many starts, stops and filling-in-the-gaps of their knowledge and skills over the years.

Occasionally, kids themselves, open a can of worms and then need a bit of help. When Chad was fifteen, he and I co-led fourth-grade boys in a bible study. The Sunday before Christmas Chad unfolded his frame (by then he towered above his dad and me much to his delight) and asked as he stood up, **"How many of you are happy at Christmas?"** Every hand shot into the air and heads nodded positively. Answers ranged from, "Yes, because I get lots of presents" to, "we buy each other one gift and then make the rest." One kid said they did a white elephant exchange; another was happy because he got to spend extra time with friends he didn't see during school. I felt, not saw, Chad's hands come solidly down on my shoulders as he walked around the circle and stopped where I was sitting on the floor amongst the kids. In a deep voice he said,

"Well, this lady and I have had some sad Christmases. When I was in a foster home she could not come see me but she made it okay..." It was unexpected. Tears pooled in my eyes and I tried blinking them away.

"Why were you in foster care?" shot back one of the boys after a burst of silence and some very rounded eyes that met mine. "That's another story," replied Chad who explained our belief in God helped us both through it. I knew we had to anchor this for the group since the door had been opened, but it was Chad's story to keep or share, so I simply responded in a quiet aside to him, "It is a fair question and deserves a one to two sentence answer." "I was adopted," was his reply. "Chad was God's gift to me," was mine. There were so many loose threads that we could have picked up—instead we pigged out on sugar, and played games. I got my Christmas gift early that year.

"People tend to think of children as weak and vulnerable, as fragile little people. In my experience, they're giants. They have immense and open hearts. Their minds can expand to encompass any reality," recalls Dr. Fred Epstein who works with 'hopeless' sick children.[58] Whatever your story is, don't be afraid to unravel the threads and discuss past experiences, and future expectations and dreams, with the kids you are parenting. They can handle the truth, as long as they know, that you love them. "I believe in you," is a very positive message for any child—but especially those with addicted parents.

Family is not about blood.
It's about who is willing to hold your hand
when you need it the most.

Unknown

12
Family Trees & Other School Landmines

In today's world of casual affairs, divorces, remarriage, same-sex or hetero-sex couple adoptions, single parents, and artificial insemination family is not an unequivocal equation. In fact the only common denominator for family, as far as schoolwork goes, is the existence of a child. Relative-based projects can register anywhere from mildly annoying to off-the-chart difficult for children with parents who are addicts or alcoholics. It depends on whether you have given them the information, and skills, to define their own family, and handle the fallout.

"First and foremost, let your student know that their lived experiences are valid and valued. They have every right to hold on to who they are, what they know, and what they live, even if sometimes they have to stop and work through differences," stated Devon Alexander, an African American teacher at Oak Park High School in a Chicago suburb. He continued, "But you also have to show them how to navigate our school culture so they can succeed."[59] Through coaching you are laying the groundwork for academic, social, and life achievements.

It all starts in preschool when kids are told to "draw your family", and continues to build as they are asked to create family trees, write about clan members' experiences in historical events (history or English) or views on finances (economics). They explore genetics (health or science) and a myriad of other tie-ins from careers to the countries that their ancestors originally came from. In addition to projects there will be parent-teacher conferences, grandparent days at some school, cards for Mother or Father's Day, as well as continual requests for parental PTO involvement or for mom/dad to be classroom helpers or special event chaperones. There are numerous forms every year for them to fill in giving their mother and father's names and emergency contact numbers. Make sure they know *whose names to put where.*

Most educators are hugely aware of culture, diversity, and family issues. They have attended sensitivity classes and have other students with backgrounds similar to your families'. A simple statement, or request, usually works. You don't want your children to stop doing schoolwork because they fall outside of a norm, are embarrassed, or don't know how to ask for help. "If you can teach a child not to look for excuses but rather to look for solutions, you're likely to raise someone who is extremely effective and extremely successful,"[60] writes 2016 Presidential candidate Dr. Ben Carson, M.D. Make life a challenge and your kids will rise to your expectations.

Defining family and exploring options is the solution

Begin now at whatever age your children are, by asking them to explain what family means to them. **Drawing a family tree would be easy today because I know who my family is...when you haven't figured that out, it's hard.** When he was ten or eleven I asked Chad if he thought of Donald as his birth dad. **"No,"** he said and shook his head. "Do you think of Brandy as your birth mom?" I continued. **"'Yah."**

Trying to help him understand his feelings, and filter them through a logic-based process, I then asked, "Why do you think of one as a birth parent and not the other?" **"Because Donald was like mean to me and [I'm] trying to get him out of my life which I can't really do because he's always going to be my birth dad...always there."** "Yah, he is," I agreed. Our conversation continued on a different track because it came out that he was worried about Donald kidnapping and hurting him. It could easily have been the jumping off place to tell him if he didn't want to include Donald in his family tree, story, or other assignment he didn't need to. We circled back, but can't tell you whether it was that day, or another. Parenting children of addicts constantly requires doing emotional triage. In that instance 'today's fear' outweighed 'tomorrow's probably' but it was just a detour, not a permanent pass.

Regardless of the assignment, your son or daughter has the right to privacy, as we continue mentioning, because moving on requires conscious decisions to let go. They shouldn't mention anyone they don't want to answer questions about, for example, an incarcerated parent no one knows about, or a sibling who does not live with them. Who they include, or exclude, will most likely vary over the years due to life changes, age, and their own feelings.

Because 'family trees' come up repeatedly over the years, talk about them specifically by mid-elementary years. Offer up the possibility of their suggesting a family circle instead of a tree, and how to explain to their teacher why they are asking. I tried once for over an hour to draw Chad's family tree, or more accurately trees, and ended up with a headache and a badly misshaped spider web, so I quit. My ex-husband and I adopted his birth mom; there is no prior family history for her. Chad's adoptive mom (me) is also his maternal grandmother. His five half-siblings on his mom's side have three different fathers; his two stepbrothers from my second marriage are really half brothers legally and full brothers in love. All of Chad's aunts, uncles and grandparents are really 'greats' but we compressed a whole generation. There's more, but you get the idea!

The logistics of diagramming the tangle of relationships for children is not only awkward but sometimes, family skeletons pop up. Chad's sixth grade Spanish teacher asked the class to create family trees using their relatives' Spanish names and titles. When Chad told him he was having difficulties, his teacher told him to just put the word divorced by his birth parents and, "not to stress." Yeah right. Chad was totally upset, and snarly, when he came home. It was ten o'clock that night before he finally told me what was bothering him. He could not remember his birth dad's last name, and he did not know where to put connecting lines. His completed tree took up 2 inches x 1.75 inches on an 8.5" x 14" paper!

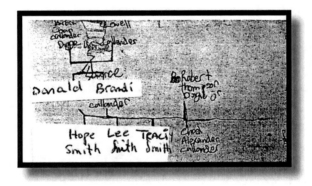

Trying to be helpful, I suggested he draw one box with me labeled as grandmother and mom. He was aghast, "And tell my whole class?" But what broke my heart, and really brought Chad down, was that after trying to add his birth parents he realized for the first time that they had never married. "Why didn't you tell me...I was...they weren't," he struggled to find the words. All I could say was, "Chad I am so sorry, and I thought you knew." I do not recall if we never talked about it, or if it had just gone over his head. I told Chad I loved him, and that he was special; that only Donald and Brandy's genes could have made him the extraordinary person he is destined to become. Hopefully, the toughest situations will play out at home, but it's not always the case.

When the assignment involves making cards or gifts for a parent no longer in their life, or no longer trusted and loved, suggest they substitute you or a favorite auntie, nana, or adult friend instead. Remind them that teachers, or youth group leaders, will help them with spelling names and titles if they are stumped. Many schools now discourage these types of projects, which I think is sad because they teach children how to be thoughtful, communicate love, and show respect. All it takes to go from painful to celebratory is for educators to add an inclusionary statement, "or for anyone who is special to you".

Often teachers unknowingly put pressure on kids to ask their mom or dad to be a parent chaperone, class helper, or participate in special projects. Come up with some realistic scenarios and have your son or daughter practice responses such as, "My dad can't chaperone the dance, but I could ask my brother who graduated last year from college," or "Mom says she's sorry but not this time," or "grandpa is a writer and he volunteered to speak at career day."

Kind of a wild child idea, but don't blow off volunteering. No one can do everything, but kids love it when you are there and when you are 'cool'. Riding a school bus at sixty, whether chaperoning an expedition to the local performing arts production or ski practice wasn't my heartbeat, but every time I did it I came away saying, "I'm so glad I went." Take a piece of advice from my nephew who was diagnosed with a life-threatening cancer in his mid-twenties and say "yes" to as many experiences as you can, at least once. After that you can choose to repeat the adventure or pass. If you're a grandparent you need to go back to things you did before and give them another try. I discovered that I still liked the sports-related connections best. From walk-a-thons to helping at track and ski meets, special events worked best for me. I still disliked the babysitting type requests, or weekly commitments that lasted an entire year.

Remind your son, daughter, or grandchildren often that you will contact teachers or youth leaders if they are having difficulty explaining their situation, but they have your support if they try on their own and blow it. *Know also when to silently step in.* Chad was given an assignment his freshman year to write a series of vignettes, over multiple months that was to be a significant part of his grade, about his relatives—and historic events. I emailed his teacher after looking at some of her comments on returned papers to tell her that because of Chad's skip generation adoption his stories might seem inconsistent or poorly thought out. Chad had written that his great grandfather (instead of great-great) on Bob's side fought in World War I while my dad, who he called grandpa not great grandpa, fought in World War II. *Bob fought in the Vietnam War and there was no one left for more recent wars.* Sometimes it's best to back off and let them work their own way through painful experiences. None of us want our kids to feel bad but it is part of growing up. If we always rescue them then when we aren't around they a) won't know how to stand up for themself, and b) won't be able to handle the really big things.

Uplift and affirm

From the time kids are little, we tell them what to do and what not to do. "Eat your cereal, don't cross the street without looking both ways, share your toys," and so on. We praise their efforts, "You're such a good baby, nice job, you told mommy you had to go potty," or clapping loudly while exclaiming, "you did it", whatever "it" is. The conversations helping them be ready for school experiences are just another step forward, "Peanut butter sandwiches aren't allowed at school because they make some children ill," or "you can't always be first on the bus." Talking about family assignments may break your heart, but to the young people you parent, if handled well, it will be just be more additions for their 'can do' or 'don't go there' lists. Granted in a perfect world these type of conversations shouldn't have to take place, but the world of addiction is far from perfect. *Competence helps develop confidence,* so once again discuss, role-play, praise, and anticipate possible and probable situations. Give your kids the gift of encouraging risk-taking.

Kids of addicts may struggle more in their early years than children from families where drugs or alcohol aren't a problem, but they develop skills and competencies that serve them well later on. Chad has aced every job interview he has had since he was fifteen because he communicates well and can quickly analyze behaviors, facts, and feelings. He moves effortlessly between all age groups. Little kids love him, he's a leader not a follower with his peers, and adults like and trust him. Chad's college application letter began with a quote from Dr. Seuss reflecting who he has become, *"Sometimes the questions are complicated and the answers are simple."* He then wrote about his life experiences, personal accomplishments, career goals, and what he could contribute as a student before he circled back to end with another quote from Seuss, *"And will you succeed? Yes, indeed, yes indeed! Ninety-eight and three quarters percent guaranteed!"*

I don't like labels because they may lump you with people that you only share one issue with.

Howard K. Smith, Broadcaster

13

Parenting Children with Special Needs

& Challenging Behaviors

Addicts' kids often have *cognitive, behavioral and physical* problems because of in utero exposure to chemicals, or because they were abused or erratically disciplined in early childhood.

"There is no known safe amount of alcohol use during pregnancy or while trying to get pregnant. There is also no safe time during pregnancy to drink. All types of alcohol are equally harmful, including all wines and beer. When a pregnant woman drinks alcohol, so does her baby," reports the Centers for Disease Control and Prevention.[61] Alcohol use can cause miscarriages, abnormal facial features, poor coordination, problems with heart, learning disabilities, and low IQ or poor reasoning and judgment skills. Recreational drug use can cause brain defects.[62] A single exposure to meth may produce long-term damage including neurodevelopmental problems[63].

Challenges for parents and relative caregivers

I agree with Desmond Tutu, "You don't choose family. They are God's gift to you, as you are to them." However, children with special needs and challenging behaviors can wear you out if you don't take regular breaks for yourself. Granted, these loving and loveable children are the youngest of wounded warriors--the victims of drugs and alcohol they've never taken--but you too will become a casualty if you don't look after yourself and focus on the gifts, not the takeaways, in life.

"Years of depression and anxiety will do as much damage to you as the drugs are doing to your loved ones."[64] So if you feel depressed, angry, or continually stressed by all the daily demands on you then please see your doctor, find a support group, call a local hotline, or talk to a counselor. Ask 'special need' organizations, caseworkers, and agencies focusing on seniors about respite care, as well as, events for you and the children.

Why you need a medical or mental health care diagnosis for your child

A professional diagnosis does several things. First, it confirms what you are seeing and feeling—or it sends you in a different direction looking for answers. Secondly, the diagnosis helps you understand the reason for the behaviors, and gives you an insight into what your son, daughter or grandchild is feeling. You'll learn what to expect both short and long term, and options for treatment and outcomes. With the problem identified, you can start finding options and workarounds. Lastly, it opens the doors for all kinds of services, including educational and financial, that persons who are differently gifted are entitled to by law. Some young ones will outgrow, or learn to manage issues, while others will need supervision and/or care for life. The 2010 Affordable Care Act makes it illegal for insurers to deny, or limit lifetime or annual essential care bene-fits. Coverage of young adults under your private insurance policy is possible until dependents reach twenty-six. If they are, or have been foster kids, call Medicaid to determine if they are eligible for benefits. *Academically* there are numerous rights and resources for any child with a disability that impacts learning, "Inclusion is a right, not a special privilege for a select few," according to the Federal Court in Oberti V. Board Of Education.

Help is available for all types and levels of disability. Be tena-cious when searching for solutions, and creative in implement-ing them. To expedite the separating of personality traits and age-related responses from treatable disorders keep a record of events and behaviors. Take it with you to all appointments. It can also help identify triggers—events or circumstances lead-ing up to inappropriate behaviors—so you can intervene and head them off. Often behaviors are common to multiple disor-ders and any one symptom is not, in itself, problematic or the basis for forming a diagnosis. Tests help identify certain disor-ders or conditions, but many are expensive, controversial, and sometimes inconclusive. Always ask about limitations, and any possible side effects for all diagnostics, recommended ther-apies, and/or pharmaceuticals.

Following are common disorders, but the list is far from all-inclusive, and the information very abbreviated:

Attention–deficit/hyperactivity Disorder (ADHD)

Once considered separate, ADD (attention deficit) and ADHD (attention hyperactivity) are now viewed as one disorder (ADHD)—a spectrum rather than an absolute. Symptoms can include impulsivity, frustration, lack of sustained attention, being constantly in motion, and impatience. All youngsters avoid things they don't want to do, such as schoolwork or chores, but these children take it to the max. They often have few friends because they miss social clues, and can be disruptive in classrooms, social settings, and family interactions. They tend to lose belongings, often forgetting simple things, while remembering complex issues that interest them.

Make eye contact with children having ADHD when talking with them, provide frequent breaks from tasks or schoolwork, stick to schedules, and avoid power struggles. Have them keep their possessions including backpacks, books, and shoes in the same place.

Request teachers who are structured, but warm, and caring. Kids with ADHD do best with smaller class sizes, short but frequent exams, and for little ones a "buddy" who they can check with to verify assignments and due dates. Encourage older students to write things down using paper or electronic calendars, and to utilize the teacher's homework pages on their school's website.

Fetal Alcohol Spectrum Disorders (FASDs)

Fetal Alcohol Syndrome (FAS), one of the most severe in the FASD spectrum, results from prenatal exposure to alcohol. "FAS is one of the leading known preventable causes of mental retardation and birth defects…Children with FAS are at risk for psychiatric problems, criminal behavior, unemployment and incomplete education. These secondary conditions are problems that an individual is not born with, but might acquire as a result of FAS."[65] A stable home life, and special education, can help them become successful students and adults by helping them learn to channel unacceptable behaviors.

Often children with FAS are short, have flat mid-face features, thin lips, heart and/or dental problems, and learning or developmental challenges. They tend to be talkative with short attention spans and short memories; they do not make cause and effect connections, or think ahead.

151

Provide structure, give single task instructions, supply a low distraction environment with no TV or music while doing homework, and remain calm. "Tell, repeat, and do" when explaining something. "It will be time for bed at eight o'clock. Five more minutes until bedtime. Bedtime."

Oppositional Defiant Disorder (ODD)

Kids diagnosed with ODD are intolerant, easily frustrated or annoyed, lose their tempers, argue, blame others for their mistakes, are vindictive and constantly challenge adult authority. They need to feel in control; life with them can seem like living in a war zone. Causes include abuse, inconsistent or extreme discipline, lack of supervision, or an imbalance of chemicals, such as serotonin, in the brain.

Assign chores that only the child is responsible for, and ones they can succeed at. Don't let them sidetrack you with, "I forgot" or other plausible sounding excuses. Consequences should be immediate and short in duration. Praise often, but honestly; do not inadvertently give the message that they are only loveable when doing good things.

Never try to fix problems when they are venting—instead make comments such as, "I hear what you are saying or makes sense to me". Offer solutions only if they ask because they will disagree with every option you put on the table. Select your skirmishes.

Collaborative parenting style, giving *limited choices*, is most effective; however, once you establish a rule, and consequences, enforce them. Understand that you are making progress even when you think you aren't. Your child is learning what happens in the world of school, work, and life. Remain low-key and unemotional when challenged. Sometimes, to stop a situation from escalating, or for your own sanity, you have to put yourself in timeout and leave the room, or house. Tell them where you are going and when you will return.

Post Traumatic Stress Disorder (PTSD)

Kids with PTSD experience anxiety brought on by trauma. Younger children may disassociate, that is, they don't remember events, lie even when truth is obvious, seem 'spaced out' or confused rather than becoming hyper-aroused because they can't physically escape. Symptoms can include bad dreams, avoidance, trouble concentrating, anger, aggressive or risky behavior, frequent irritation and flashbacks (ages 5-12 may remember events out of chronological order or mix things up).

In second grade, Chad's school was locked down because of a nearby shooting. There were police and helicopters and the school counselor ended up talking to him for forty-five minutes. "He was visibly scared and jumped at every noise," according to his teacher. He had told the janitor that his dad was wearing a black mask and was on the edges of the playground with a gun. "He did it." Factually, Chad hadn't been outside but his PSTD was triggered big time.

Parents and teachers need to remain calm, in control, and be as physically nurturing as is appropriate and the child will allow. Encourage art and creative outlets. Physical activity is good for overall health and helps prevent depression, but aggressive contact sports may ramp up heart rates, cause shortness of breath, or trigger other bodily symptoms associated with PTSD and could end up increasing anxiety. There isn't adequate scientific data at this time to determine if sports are positive or negative.[66] So try new things, but follow your child's lead and change courses if things don't work out.

Cognitive-Behavioral Therapy encourages adolescents to talk about their memory of the trauma and introduces techniques to lessen stress and worry with added assertiveness training (be safe, remove self from area, get help). Other approaches depending on their age include play therapy; eye movement desensitization; and reprocessing (EMDR) or exposure (talking repeatedly about the feelings, emotions and thoughts associated with the trauma to lessen their impact).

Heart hurt:
A picture of Brandy that Chad drew after a visitation.
Age six.

Reactive Attachment Disorder (RAD)

RAD often results when crying infants weren't changed when wet, fed when hungry, or shown affection. Many had multiple caregivers, including relatives and foster parents. These children often don't make eye contact and are superficially charming with no, or poor, boundaries. They can be clingy, talkative, and have trouble forming friendships. They may cry incessantly and cannot be consoled. Cruelties to animals or other children, being accident prone, self-destructive, or rejecting physical touch are other characteristic behaviors.

When parenting kids diagnosed with RAD, offer physical comfort and support; be consistent, always saying what you will do and doing what you say. These children had to rely on themselves to survive; they developed no empathy or conscience and parenting/teaching them can be taxing. It may be a long journey, but the damage can be undone if the child learns to trust you and feels safe.

Ask for teachers who post rules as well as consequences and rewards, and who follow through with them every time. The children react positively to structure, with reoccurring daily activities. Teachers who give them choices such as, "Do you want to color at your desk or the group activity table? Would you rather do all the problems now or save the last two for homework?" achieve the best results.

Treatments and services; rights and concerns

"Don't overlook the importance of maintaining a strong relationship with your pediatrician, and regardless if you have private or public health care insurance, know your benefits. Stress the safety of all family members when requesting help," says Tamara White Bakewell, Project Coordinator of Oregon Health & Science University's Family to Family Health Information Center in Portland, Oregon. And she adds, "Consider denials from your health plan as a request for more information. By asking, "What do you need to get to 'yes'," you keep the dialog open and often find a mutually acceptable solution whether you are dealing with physical, cognitive, learning, or emotional disabilities.

"Children [with] *developmental disabilities* make the most progress when they are recipients of aggressive early intervention programs. Early intervention plans are usually the result of one of two different processes. The *Individualized Family Service Plan, or IFSP*, is directed at the youngest children [birth through two and often happens with in-home services], and is geared toward helping them reach developmental goals. The *Individualized Education Plan, or IEP*, is focused on preparing the child to learn alongside their non-disabled peers in the school system."[67] Throughout their school career all children with *learning disabilities,* by law, are entitled to special services according to the Individuals with Disabilities Education Act (IDEA). *A free and appropriate IEP must be developed and implemented by your school district.*

Medications

No one wants to encourage unnecessary medications—least of all anyone with addictions in their family. It is a valid concern, shared by many today, that youth with behavior issues may be misdiagnosed and that medications, such as Ritalin® or Prozac®, are being over prescribed.[68] Reputable doctors and therapists proceed cautiously, and welcome second opinions. Talk openly about your reservations—including proclivity towards alcohol or drug addictions.

Ken Ensroth M.D., a psychiatrist and Medical Director for Child and Adolescent Psychiatry at Providence Willamette Falls Medical Center, represents the opposing viewpoint saying that ADHD is more often under-diagnosed than treated. Feeling that the right medications make huge changes in a child's life he stipulates, "Medicating a child should always be done on a trial basis; if it doesn't seem to be working, or if your son experiences unpleasant side effects, then the drug or dosage should be changed or discontinued. One of the advantages of stimulant ADHD medications is that they take effect very quickly. You should be able to tell within days whether it's helping or causing side effects."[69] You know your child best. Keep communications with child and doctor open and follow your instincts. Don't be afraid to ask questions or demand answers.

Alternative approaches

Naturopathic remedies and therapeutic treatments including retraining brain and muscular functions are highly regarded by some--scoffed at by others. "Non-medication therapies often include adjusting the demands placed on children, sometimes called environmental management," explains Michael Goldstein, a Utah pediatric neurologist and former vice president of the American Academy of Neurology. "It means changing the expectations of parents and teachers to more closely conform to the child's abilities— for example, giving simple directions and supervising the child's responses."[70]

Kids are not always capable of being their own gatekeeper. **When I used to get so angry it was like I was drunk and didn't know what was going on. Later I'd think, "What just happened?" I didn't know how I had gotten to the point of being out of control half of the time.** Family counseling is helpful in that difficult conversations can be mediated by a neutral party, someone who often will back you up or suggest alternative approaches or compromises. Mutually improved communication skills lead to further breakthroughs at home, and set up opportunities for life-long bonding.

Sharing information

Whether you are just starting or years into parenting, and whatever your family's past or current situation, you can control what information to share with whom. Doctors, therapists, and private practice counselors need information to correctly diagnose and treat problems. Educators need information to ensure your child qualifies for special needs programs, and for them to get the financial aid they need to provide those services. Knowing about behavioral issues that impact classroom learning and social interaction can help teachers spot problems and appropriately intervene. *Just reiterating, they do not need to know everything, even if they ask.* It's a lesson Chad and I learned the hard way.

The same week I told Chad's third-grade teacher, at the new school where we had just moved, that he had been abused; I received a call from their school counselor accusing Chad of inappropriate sexual contact with a girl classmate. Supposedly he trapped her against the playground fence during recess and was rubbing up against her. He had never been in any trouble at his old school and his best friend was a neighbor girl who frankly out-batted and out-ran all the boys in the neighborhood; she shared Chad's enthusiasm for playing with miniature power-rangers and plastic swords. Nothing remotely sexual ever occurred. I was totally freaked out.

The school counselor finally admitted after relentless questioning by me, that there was no complaint from the classmate or her family. In fact both Chad and the girl, when questioned separately by the principal and a teacher, had said they were playing chase and ran into each other. No adult had observed the encounter, and I am not quite sure who, or what, prompted the accusation but I was told, "Sexually abused children have a propensity to be sexually aggressive." Once I clarified it was physical not sexual abuse that Chad had experienced as a toddler, the school counselor said, "Then there is no problem," meaning I guess, that Chad wasn't a predator in the making.

Well, she was wrong. There was a problem but it wasn't Chad's background or his behavior. The school staff created the false labeling and accusation problem—but I had inadvertently opened the door. I over-shared information with a teacher who didn't need to know Chad's past. Later I realized how often I did this in his early years simply because I was concerned what people would think of my having a young child at my age, and I was embarrassed by Brandy's drug and parenting choices. The teacher had shared information that was meant to be private with others, and the telling and retelling lead to false conclusions and false allegations that could have resulted in consequences that stayed with Chad for life.

Following the advice of Chad's private-practice counselor and my attorney, I demanded that the incident file, and all notes, be shredded so there was no documentation in any way describing him as having been physically or sexually abused. I requested copies of his files for years to ensure nothing was slipped back in. I told Chad to be careful of coming in physical contact with any other student—framing it in the context of personal space—not sexual perversion. I never again shared information without a really, really, really well thought out reason that, if not shared, could have hurt Chad.

Chad never received any special education or counseling services at school. His help came from outside resources that were paid for by the state when he was in foster care, and myself after that. This does not mean that school services are not helpful or that school staff is not competent or caring, but rather that they should be supplemental or supportive not all-inclusive. Many families do depend entirely on school systems to provide all the services their child needs and this is not realistic. School budgets and resources for special needs are limited. Take heart, in that, there are a number of really good and affordable community and health programs available. Check out resources in the appendix or again call your caseworker, ask your pediatrician, go on-line or ask other families for resources and references.

Often information *does* need to be shared with educators. For example, when Chad entered kindergarten his teacher needed to know that his birth dad had a temper, that I had court-ordered custody, and abduction was a very real possibility. Also, Chad was exhibiting PTSD symptoms. Due to a series of staffing changes, Chad had the same teacher for three years so the knowledge of his home life was very contained. By the time he was in the third grade, and we changed school districts, his birth dad lived thousands of miles away and his birth mom was in recovery so safety was no longer an immediate concern. When Bob and I married and left on a week honeymoon six weeks into the school year, all I should have shared was "I'm Chad's guardian and here is a note authorizing only my sister to pick him up for any reason while I'm gone. This is her number, and she will show you her identification."

159

As Chad got older, he chose who and what he wanted to share. **There are things I told friends, who turned out not to be real friends, and later I wished I had kept them to myself. It was easy to talk to my best friend and Jessica. Both helped me a lot.**

Over all, we were blessed with people who helped Chad grow into a healthy adult, and me survive. I want to emphasize that educators are dedicated people. As professionals they have huge demands on them as a result of laws, government mandates, cultural changes, and budget constraints. Occasionally, as people, they share information they shouldn't—but I think it's the exception not the rule. Normally, confidences lead to better understanding and positive learning experiences for children. Occasionally, educators' confidential conversations are overheard, or records that should be secured are not. So as a precaution, especially until you know the system and the staff, consider carefully what you want to divulge.

IEP meetings are more productive if you come prepared. Bring copies of evaluations, vital records, questions you want answered, and services you are requesting. Take a family member, or friend, with you to take notes and remind you of anything you are forgetting. Focus on immediate goals, not past history. Ask for written confirmation of everything decided including prognosis, recommended programs, responsible names, and promised time frames.

Federal law gives you, as a parent or guardian, the right to receive a copy of all *school records—primary and secondary-*-for children under the age of eighteen within 45 days of written request. Facts such as a failed class, documented incidents of misbehavior, or suspension can be challenged for bias or incompleteness – or you can ask to attach a note of explanation or disagreement. Unsubstantiated opinions such as "Nora is a slow learner," or "Enrique is a trouble maker" are not acceptable and you should insist they be destroyed. For documented incidents in your student's file that happened outside of the school's jurisdiction, such as social network bullying or sexting, seek legal counsel. These areas are in flux.

School incidents

"What used to be, in our day, a trip to the principal's office now lands you in court,"[71] *says Texas Chief Justice, Wallace Jefferson.* Children have enough trouble trying to grow up without negative stereotypes, or false accusations, clouding their future so personally show up at school for any disciplinary incident. Listen, but do not comment, before hearing both the school's side and your child's side. "I will get back to you tomorrow," gives you time to sort out facts while talking about feelings and consequences with your child. It also lets the school know that you are a concerned, caring, and involved parent. Even if your student is suspended, or expelled, don't change your approach. Be polite but ask to schedule another meeting for the next day, or soon after. If your child is at fault, waiting a day to acknowledge it isn't going to change the facts. If your child is not at fault, or you feel the discipline is arbitrary or inappropriate given the facts, do not roll over—*educators are not always right.* Go up the ladder of command if necessary; however, pick your battles and explain why to your son, daughter, or grandkid. *Questionable incidents can become teachable moments. Children need to know that life is not fair. Model, and explain, to your offspring how to effectively challenge undeserved accusations, communicate respectfully when rebutting arguments, and sometimes how to buck up and live with undeserved consequences. What you don't want is to let a disorder or disability, or an addicted family member's negative reputation, subtract from the quality of your child's life or limit their future potential.*

Celebrate baby steps and big milestones

A major obstacle for a lot of people nowadays is childhood abuse, and the effects and challenges it brings later in life. Physical abuse and bad parenting by my birthparents, although I didn't realize it at the time, was the biggest challenge I have had to overcome. As a result of my childhood trauma, I had to go through multiple counseling experiences to try and clear up my anger, stress, and fears. Ultimately, every counselor explained the same thing; I needed to conquer the obstacles in my head before I could overcome them in reality. I took this to heart and worked hard with my adoptive parents, and with my friends, to become a better person.

As a parent continually ask yourself what your child needs from you, or others, right now. Sometimes it's medical, other times it's academic, but often it's a practical workaround. For example, "Students with learning disabilities are not effective note takers...often unable to identify the important informa-tion...write fast enough...make sense of their notes after the lecture."[72] The learning disability website where I found this information targets educators, but you can personalize their tips concerning a range of subjects from 'Accommodations and modifications' to 'Reading to help your student do better in the classroom and with homework'. Many school districts offer study skills classes at various levels, or you can look for private resources. Educate yourself on legally required accommoda-tions that you can request, such as having your student being provided written or electronic notes in college, or being given verbal, rather than written, tests at all levels.

It does take a village to raise a child—but make darn sure you hand pick who lives in your child's village, or that you monitor and buffer the influences that are neutral to negative. Savor every victory--one good day at school, chores done without asking, and even the transition from angry at everything, to a typical annoying teen "whatever" attitude. Look for positives, praise your kids or grandchildren, and pat yourself on the back.

Not environment, not heredity, but personal response is the final determining factor in our lives. And herein lies our area of responsibility.

Martin Luther King

14
Teens: Technology, Sex and Other Things that Drive Parents Crazy

"All three of our adopted sons had in utero drug and alcohol exposure and that causes organic issues. Our nineteen-year-old is for all emotional and practical purposes fifteen," says a Utah mother of eight who I'll call Sandra. "He has a good heart, and the rest of the kids love him and miss him since he moved last week, but he has no impulse control and little common sense. He was totally a victim of the system with so many placements and so much physical, sexual, and emotional abuse by foster parents and other foster kids from his birth to age seven when we got him. *We've poured everything into him that we possibly could, including extensive counseling, but now he has to decide who he's going to be.*"

Teenage years are difficult, they are transitional—the storm before adulthood. When you take over sole parenting in teen years of an addict's child it's even tougher because they've lived with dysfunction for so long, rational thinking and acting makes no sense to them. Alcoholics change jobs and 'homes'

163

frequently, and they think every bad that happens to them is someone else's fault. Consequently, their *teens may be street smart, but academically and relationally challenged. They gravitate to other teens in similar situations.*

We're going to talk about parenting teens of users as well as teens in general. Every child deserves a dad like NASCAR driver Brian Scott who vowed to the three-year-old daughter of the woman he married, "I promise to always hold your hand and skip with you down the street and bring comfort to your life. I vow to make you say your prayers before you eat. I promise to read you stories at night and to always tuck you in real tight. I vow to show you how a man should treat a woman in my relationship with your mother. And above all else, I vow to protect you, care for you, and love you forever."[73]

However, instead of bedtime stories, prayers and butterfly kisses, kids with addicted parents, often see and hear sex acts. "Aunties" or "uncles" come and go, and they may have been fondled, ogled, or raped by them. Violence was as likely directed at them, as it was to their mom or dad. Add in today's de-personalizing of family and peer relationships through technology, and these teens need you to increase the quantity of quality time you spend with them. *They need you to fight for them, not with them.*

Today's culture

If fifty is the new forty, then the new thirteen is more like eight or nine. **The average age of puberty in American girls today is nine and a half.**[74] A lot of girls' clothes today are designed to give off a sassy, or sexy look, that can quickly turn slutty if it's worn too tight, too low cut, or too short. You are the gatekeeper for what comes in, and goes out of your home. However, pop-in visits to school might leave you with your mouth hanging open as you see what other kids wear, and what your own child has on verses what they left the house wearing in the morning. You can't put off "the sex talk", or "the drug talk" or any culturally significant talk until high school...not even until middle school. Sadly, you have to start discussions from the moment children can hear, and absorb, what's playing in the background as well as what's being said directly to them. You have to prepare yourself, and your kids, for the teen years long before they celebrate those double-digit birthdays.

The average child, eight years and older, logs over seven hours a day of screen time—TV, videogames, computer, movies or whatever. They're exposed to 25,000 TV ads alone each year—with over 40 percent of them being from shows intended for older audiences."[75]   What was R rated in the 1990's is often PG-13 today and even nightly news shows have hostesses showing a lot of cleavage as they throw pictures of beheadings, school shootings, and hostage situations up on the screen.

A really big problem is that kids are being taught by movies like *Fifty Shades of Gray,* TV shows, music videos, and video games about sex. Monogamous sex, or waiting until after marriage, is shown as boring; sex experimentation, and partner swapping, as cool. In real life, teens would probably be in jail for a lot of the things portrayed as a normal sex life. TV shows do have a rating system to show what age of kids should be able to watch them. However, ratings are becoming more and more lenient. For example, the rating of 'TV-MA' can vary between a show that has some sexual references and drug use to a show that is basically pornography.

You have to talk about sex in general before you can talk about sex and technology. But you have to put restrictions on technology—setting time limits and talking about pushing buttons without asking mom or dad-- as soon as kids reach for your cell, tablet, or the remote. Today one in three kids between the ages of three and five have their own tablet; they grow up tech wise, so you always need to know a bit more than they do about devices, apps, and software.

As for sex, what you say to little ones depends on their knowledge level based on their past experience and exposure. For teens, you pretty much have to lay it all on the line because it's openly flaunted on media and openly available everywhere today. In college, you see people having sex in their rooms with the doors open all the time. From what my half sisters have shared, and posted on social media, I'm guessing it's like that when living with an addict. When a child starts having sex at twelve, you know it's going to be hard to convince them a few years later to stop. Admonishments like "employers almost always do Internet searches and can pull up anything you ever posted—pictures or words", go right over their heads.

Physical sex

Teens are hormone driven and frequently confuse sex with romance, love, or approval. The older your child, the more direct you have to be in confronting this flawed logic because any leverage you have over how they act is rapidly disappearing. According to researchers at the University of Virginia, youth who are romantically involved in seventh and eighth grade end up having less social relationship skills and more drug, alcohol, and criminal activities.[76] Anytime you talk about sex, be straightforward and don't sugar coat the information or consequences of unprotected physical or cyber sex. Teens, and even tweens, probably know what you know about sex—in fact they may know more, but our twisted society doesn't show them the consequences of casual sex.

Not debating sex education theories or morality. Some studies show that teens told to have 'safe sex' are actually more likely to show restrain than those told to 'abstain'. Other studies dispute it. Teens often do what they are told not to, just to prove that they can. I will say there is such thing as 'safe sex'. It can be safe sex if you use condoms and the pill, have only one partner who has never had sex with anyone before you, and you are mature enough to handle not only the physical, but emotional ups and downs. But realistically nothing is totally safe—especially if either partner is lying about their past, or about birth control and condom use.

Many teens today consider casual sex a replacement for dating, and think that oral sex isn't really sex. Sending selfies of their naked body or genitals via smart phones, or skyping intimate poses and sexual acts seems like no big deal to them. Teens trust their girl friend, or boy friend, to keep confidential pictures and texts private. They aren't prepared to deal with the consequences when they don't. Apps like Snapchat® give them a false sense of security since images disappear almost instantaneously—but the recipient can capture and re-share. As a parent, it's your job to teach the physical stuff and also personal health, safety and moral context.

A lot of values-based messages can't be delivered under the umbrella of sex without push back, but they can be shown by how you live life; by teen years it's really the only avenue that leaves an impact. Textbook biology and health classes that begin in grade school will fill in most anatomy gaps, but they need to hear about all aspects of sex from you first. They need straight talk on intercourse, oral, and anal. Discuss homosexuality, regardless of your personal views, because schools and society today promote it through 'discover yourself' curriculum, and 'right to work, right to marriage' laws.

If your teen is already sexually active, "Sit down and say you need to be completely honest with each other so you can help," suggests Chad's wife, Jessica, who just graduated from college. "Be upfront and don't judge...you don't want them to feel bad, just learn to respect themselves...and you want to keep communication lines open. Ask if they have had sex, and if it is more than general vaginal sex. All ways can affect a person mentally, as well as physically, and impact their self-esteem. Share knowledge about STI's (sexually transmitted infections) and STD's (Sexually transmitted diseases), prevention, birth control, annual checkups." Then follow-up by taking them for a physical and birth control (realism not approval)—and do it for both sexes. Once sexually active most teens, even when changing environments, continue being sexually active especially if it gets them what they want: acceptance by the cool crowd and dates.

Cyber sex

Discuss sex trolls on the Internet, cyber and real life stalkers, cyber bullying, and cyber predators. Sexual perverts pretend to be teens on-line and often ask for pictures, make suggestive or lewd comments, try to meet up in person while pushing to keep the relationship secret—by making secrecy seem intimate and their 'relationship' too special to share. Stress the importance of not 'friending' anyone they don't know personally, and not posting where they live, go to school, vacation, or activities they are involved in. GPS software makes any picture in the world easily tracked and locations pinpointed—period.

Let your son/daughter/grandchild know that they can talk to you anytime, about anything, because some things are too serious, too dangerous, and also too scary to handle on their own. *If they mess up remind them that everyone does, but how they handle it will define them as a person going forward.* Help with damage control including "some phrases she [he] can use when [he]she gets comments and looks from other kids. Better to have her [him] say in a kind of sarcastic tone: "God, I can't believe I was so stupid" or "I know, what was I thinking?" When teens own their behavior it gives other kids less to say, and they'll just have to move on."[77] If it's into the realm of school involvement, adult predators, or legal charges contact the police and an attorney.

Explain that 'zero tolerance' means a criminal investigation and probably probation, juvenile detention, jail or having to register as a sex offender for life if they initiate, forward, or store videos or pictures of a minor engaged in sexual activities—including nudity. Doesn't matter if they started the chain unintentionally, as a prank, or if someone else used their electronic device without their knowledge.

Checking versus monitoring

With all of the information out there about how to unblock a phone or websites, personal checking is more useful than monitoring apps. Let your kids know that you will be looking at their text messages often. If there are deleted messages (messages that are missing in a chain of texts), then you know to ask why and discuss their answer. Ditto for if calls were made, or received, late at night. If they turn their tablet/phone over, or shut their laptop when you come in the room, then check it out on the spot.

You can also examine browser histories on their computer and tablets. When it comes to pictures/videos, do not allow your children to store photos in a vault app—even if you have the password. Again, the best security comes from knowing as much, or more, than your kids do about devices, apps and software. Our high school prohibited downloading games or social media, but we all knew how to circumvent the checks and during class there would be thirty of us all playing the same game or posting on Facebook.

If you walk in on a TV show or movie that your teen is watching alone, or with friends, and whether it's mildly or wildly inappropriate, you have to decide if it's better to turn it off and talk, or sit down, watch, and comment. "Talk about sex in a real way: that it's fun, funny, sexy, awkward…all the things that the entertainment industry gets so well," says Lawrence Swiader the Director of Bedsider that was launched by The National Campaign to Prevent Teen and Unplanned Pregnancy three years ago. "How can we possibly compete with all of the not-so-healthy messages about sex if we have to speak like doctors and show stale pictures of people who look like they're shopping for car insurance?"[78] Some video games can be just as suggestive and need your continual attention also.

Young teens don't need smart phones and there's nothing wrong with limited text and data plans—easiest way to monitor time, if not content. If you see the same number repeatedly and don't recognize it, try goggling it. Be the good example. Don't text/call/email kids at school unless really important and even then not during class times. If it's an emergency call the office. *Don't call or text them when they are driving—and let them know not to check caller ID or answer. Instead, expect a call as soon as they arrive at their destination. Give them kudos for not answering until they were safe.*

In my opinion, young teens do need smartphones. Not for what they would use it for, but for the social stigma attached to not having one. Flip phones are barely around anymore, and if a child has one, it can cause bullying and more.

170

Reputations and respect

To an adolescent, being "liked" on social media is the new measure of popularity and popularity equates to, in their world, respect. So talking to them about reputations and implications means you have to talk in their terms. Is a 'like' real, or just something everyone does? Do they ever 'like' when they don't mean it? And, "Who was popular last year? Are they still? Why?" Then flip to the negative and ask (I hate these terms but teens use them), "Who is known as a 'skank' or 'ho' in your school?" Their responses obviously guide where the conversation goes next, but often transitions into sexual behaviors and/or clothes.

The story of clothes plays out in most homes beginning when toddlers start pulling on their own princesses' gowns or batman underwear. Clothes reflect who a person is, and often with teens, they use clothes to fit in—or for their shock value. So be prepared to have to leap over a generational disconnect to get to a universal truth. "Talk about how stereotypes are attached to each style of clothing, and how other people judge based on their perception of each style," says Jessica. "But first, update yourself by looking at the general styles that people are wearing, what's in popular teen magazines, and what's in stores, because even from when I went to high school the styles have changed. When you shop, set up outfits through compromise. Have them try on one outfit they want, and one you pick out. Just balance it. For girls, push tights, socks, and leggings, even shorts with lace on the edge to wear under other outfits. Thick belts, or high waist bottoms work with shorter tops." **Keep your negative comments brief, "Too short, not for school," and expand the positives, "That really makes you look older (taller) whatever."** With boys you obviously have other issues such as too tight, holes in sexually explicit spots, etc. *Clothes are temporary, so have the conversation and be prepared to rehash it again and again because what you see is a visual of what they are thinking.*

Know your teen's friends and dates. Meet their parents. The same goes for anyone driving them places, chaperoning a party or sleepover, or otherwise spending time with them. **Pepper was totally upset when I plopped myself down on the couch with her and her boyfriend. She took it that I didn't trust her, which was true given her past and the things she said, but she never saw that a larger part was because I cared. I wanted a better life for her, more than she had with her birthparents, and I wanted her to want to be respected. I wanted her to be safe.**

If they want to go someplace that you feel uneasy about, ask how or what--not why--questions. "Let me think about it," is a perfectly good answer as long as you do get back to them shortly; "no" isn't an open invitation to debate. 90% of messages delivered actually come from non-verbal actions such as rolled eyes or clenched jaws. Watch theirs; control yours. No harm, no foul in listening to conversations in the back seat, or your family room.

We had an unbreakable rule that even after Bob or I had met his friends, regardless if Chad had his cell phone, we needed the address and phone number where he was going to be. Plans change, emergencies happen, and accountability is part of all relationships.

Make your home youth friendly

I laughed out loud when I heard Joyce Meyer say she had a sign in her home, "I child proofed my home but they still keep getting in." Sometimes it feels that way when your house is crawling with teens, but by having the house where adolescences congregate to make salsa for Spanish class, or to practice for the band they formed, you know where your kids are, and who they're with. When you offer warm cookies after school, host a Super Bowl party with frequent wandering in and out so you can laugh over ads, or encourage impromptu pizza making, or join in the ugly sweater run, midnight madness bowling, or local bike challenges you're helping a whole neighborhood see that fun doesn't have to involve drugs, sex, or other risky behaviors.

Ryan, my best friend, and I spent a lot of time at both of our homes. My other friends knew they could be at our house after school or frequently overnight, but a few kids that I hung out with for a short time my mom closely monitored and then, most often her answer was, "No we're busy, or not for a whole weekend, or no that's not a concert venue appropriate for kids your age." During the early years of high school my mom and I clashed a lot and tensions were high, but in the end it all worked out.

Drugs and alcohol

You'd think kids of alcoholics and addicts wouldn't try alcohol or drugs, but like all teenagers they believe, "I can handle it." Reinforce that no drugs including alcohol is the law for them as a minor, and complying is one of the ways they earn the right to go out on weekends, keep their driver's license, etc. Talk about their genetic risks, and that you'll pick them up— no questions asked if they ever need you to. Tell them they can always use you for an excuse, "Just got a text from dad— have to go."

Schools are a breeding ground for drug deals; it happened every day in the halls at my old high school but really it started in middle school. Some parents don't want to think so, but it's equally bad in private and public high schools. Alcohol and drug parties are all around, your teens have to learn to deal with it and be strong enough to walk away. In college, no matter what, your kids will be exposed. You raise your kid and just hope they don't come back with an addiction. By that age they have to figure it out on their own.

What to do if your teen is using

First try to confirm it by looking in their room, backpack, or car--sorry there is no privacy when drugs are involved. If you find pot or other drugs, and it's a small amount and the first time, you may want to dispose of them down the toilet which is not good for water supplies but better than your child's health or life. Don't carry it on your person to dispose of, or hide it. If it's a lot, they are probably dealing. If they have a lot of extra money, be suspicious. Either way you need to talk. Don't buy excuses, and don't shrink from giving natural consequences. Stop giving them money. Pay their bills directly, including depositing money into their school lunch funds. Make them work for their cash and then you monitor where it's going. Get them counseling; call "211" for more information and to find out what services are available in your town.

If they've tried counseling or rehab unsuccessfully then you may have to kick them out, especially if you have other minors in your home, or call the police. When they are underage you can be held legally responsible for harm they do, or laws you knowingly let them break.

Teens turn into adults

One of the best things that happened to me was joining ROTC my freshman year in college. In ROTC if I had gotten one MIP, posted sexual pictures, or otherwise harmed my reputation, I would have been kicked out. Anytime teens experience new types of freedom there's risk of them going off the deep end—but letting them do something they want, and letting them know you trust and have confidence in them, builds up their self-esteem and a desire not to let you down.

Teen years don't last forever, and most kids make it through with just a few scrapes and scars. Use rules when you have to, but know that relationship and trust are the lasting foundation builders.

Don't compare the inside of your family to the outside of others.

Meagan, Devine LCPC

15
When Children of Addicts Grow Up

Until the kids you are parenting today are grown, your patience and parenting skills will be taxed to the max because addictions, and their fallout, are ugly. Babies of alcoholics and drug users have more physical and emotional scars than their parents have tattoos (not that tattoos are bad...in fact Chad has several). Teens are layers of attitude and facades. And you are dealing with the rest of the things life throws at you.

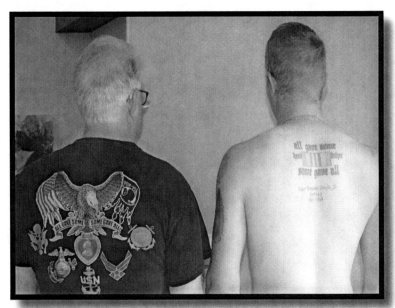

Father/son Tattoo & T-shirt: **All gave some. Some gave all.**

I read somewhere that humans need three things: someone to love, something to do, and some reason for living. Parenting fulfills all of them instantaneously, so you're on a roll. There are no guarantees in life, but story after story from the sober parent, grandparents, and the grown children of addicts who were rescued, say 'life is better than good'. *All you have to do is hang on.* The once little ones will be free to write new beginnings to the story of 'the rest of their life' because you are exposing them to the flip side of alcohol and drugs. You're giving them the possibility of a different future than their genetic inclinations, or life experiences, would seem to have dictated. *Some will self-destruct, but their choices are on them. Most will turn out wonderfully normal in this crazy screwed up world.*

Future family relationships

Once kids are grown, you will be free to decide how you want to spend the rest of your life, and it begins with--no surprise— family. For fourteen chapters Chad and I have encouraged you to severe relationships with drug users and alcoholics, or strongly control and limit them. So, when the minors become adults, you and they, face new decisions. Will you want to reconnect if you also disconnected, or changed your relationship with the user? Will the 'child of' the addict or alcoholic want to try to re-connect? Will you help them or try to block it? And, how will you handle the barrage of mixed feelings?

The addict and you

If your loved one is still using, then I don't see any reason to contact them, but that's just me. If they are recovering and sober, it's up to you—all stories are different. Sometimes, it's good to be able to finally say, "You hurt me, and you hurt your kids but guess what? Our lives are now good, and I forgive you. I know you were hurt also." Then *their* reaction, and *your* heart, suggests whether to stay or go.

It took me years to figure out that *if you bring an addict back to the same family, neighborhood, job, and friends where they got in trouble, then it is crazy to think they have any chance of permanently changing. It's a setup for failure. If you reconnect you absolutely have to let them be the person they've become—regardless of the time span in between. You need to let them exist in their own environment.* You cannot expect them to magically fit back into the mode of being a loving son, daughter, spouse, and mom or dad. You cannot expect them to suck up their emotions, overcome their problems, conquer their fears, and get on with *their* life—on *your* terms. You have to accept them where they are, and decide if re-entry in a one-on-one relationship with you, and/or total family immersion, will hurt *anyone* or help *everyone*. Never use relationships as a weapon or leverage; expect miracles, but accept less.

I shared this "ah ha" moment shortly after recognizing it with inmates. After my speech a young man from, Minnesota, told me that it was not until his mom went to Al-Anon that she finally got it. He said that he had been fighting just to survive. It was too big of a jump, too soon. *"My going back and living at home was too much pressure for me."* Recovering addicts with felony records may have had a very difficult time getting a good job. Socially, they have probably gravitated to others in recovery, or at work, and while reconnecting with their family may be important to them, it's also scary. Too much togetherness, too soon, is not productive. The longer the separation has been, the more the nucleus of the family has shifted and the addict is on the outside looking in. *They* may not want to reconnect. If they do, then it's going to take time to re-establish trust on everyone's part, and to forge new relationship roles. Depending on separation time frames and damage, this could take a few months or it could take years.

The alcoholic or addict and their adult child

Don't assume that how you feel is how the child you are parenting now will feel, or that they will be totally open in sharing with you what they are thinking. You may want to bridge the gap between you and the user, and their children may not, or vice versa. The human desire to know, and bond with, biological parents is incredibly strong. When Pepper was with us, Chad took her to visit Brandy one day and even though Pepper was not happy sharing Brandy's attention, Chad told me, "I just wanted to have a few good memories with Brandy." I am sad that things didn't work out differently between Chad and Brandy, and even though I stayed pretty neutral, I was done at exactly the same time that Chad severed ties forever. I don't know if that syncing up is typical, I suspect it is not.

Human desire for family is huge, and that's what can really hurt or really help you through these times. You may want to have some good memories, but with that be prepared to get hurt at the same time. That's what I had to do, and I'm okay with that. Sacrifices will be made, and sometimes they get pretty bad, but it's important to find where your balance is in order to be happy. It's always situational. Both of you have to go halfway--each has to give the same amount or you are going to have an unbalanced relationship. The addict has to be willing to acknowledge that they got themselves into the problem, and they have had to get themselves out. You, their adult child, probably can't be there for them emotionally—at least not at first. You are still hoping they will take care of your needs.

If your kids reconnect and you don't want to, don't make them feel guilty. And don't take the reuniting personally. Forget interrogations and settle for what they volunteer. As parents, I think a bit of our heart always hurts just a little when our role changes whether it's through marriage, or something else, until you realize that jealousy is a killer, and mercy a multiplier, when it comes to love. *However, we (for the last time) do not know your story. For the health of everyone—no one-- not you, the addict or the grown child--can fake feelings.* You cannot go back and undo; you cannot pretend to be a family that nothing bad has happened to. Instead, you have to talk about the past, the present, and then eventually your relationship may grow into something more 'normal' in the future. It might not. You may totally not want to try.

I do want to say that throughout the book you've read a number of very insightful quotes by Brandy during times of sobriety and a lot of little vignettes that capture things that I remember, or Chad remembers, that weren't so good. I think it's critical to point out that we are sharing the impact we felt as a mother and son of someone who abused alcohol and drugs in the hope that you can side-step the whiplash of mistakes made, including my mistake of not disconnecting early on. There is nothing "to forgive"; all the hurt, all the anger is gone. Most days I just don't let myself think, feel, or wonder about where Brandy is, and what she's doing.

There isn't a day that goes by that I don't think about wanting my birth dad to someday to see me as a successful father, maybe a brewer as a career, and as husband. I want him to wish, "Why did I ruin my chance so many years ago?" As for Brandy, there was a point in my life where I determined that I had to face what happened head on. I decided two things, that if anyone asked me about what happened, I would tell them, and that I couldn't wait around for Brandy to come back and be my mom, or even my mommy. She couldn't parent me in any way. However, at that time, I was open to her being a 'mom-friend'. If you look at bad mother-child relationships, where the child is still growing up and the mother should be raising the child but you see that the mother is too much of a friend, this is what I mean by 'mom-friend'. For awhile I stayed loosely in touch waiting for her to make the move of doing things like inviting me over for lunch in between my college classes, or she and her boyfriend wanting to play video games with me after school. It's things like that that showed me she was in recovery, and made me want to go the extra distance to be a friend to her. Then, with Pepper, it all blew up. But it turned out okay because Brandy showed me, that drugs or alcohol aside, she isn't a person I want in my life. She said things to me that she can't take back, and I can't ever forget. The sad thing is my half-sisters are really screwed up because of her, but that isn't my story to tell. However, I hope there is someone else placed in their lives to help them.

I read this article about a lady in our hometown that helped raise money for a student in a lower income school in a nearby city. The high school senior had lived with his great grandmother until his freshman year when he had to move, and that move left him lost and not doing well. After discovering, as a sophomore, a love for music he turned himself around and eventually snagged a full scholarship to St. Francis in New York. *"I want out of here...I want something bigger for myself,"* he told a reporter.[79] So the lady gathered together community support and got the young student a driver's license so he could board a plane to get to school, money to pay the baggage fee for the new luggage he was given to hold his new clothes, a cell phone and $450 in gift cards because he had zero cash.

One of the lady's comments referenced her own son, *"He was 23 and drowning in meth. I tried to help him for so long. I've prayed. I've cried. I've been on meds. I've put him in treatment. I've been through all those things and I couldn't do anything else. And if I can't help my own kids..."* then added the reporter, *"you help someone else's child."* I hope that when you write 'finished' to the end of your child-rearing days, your story will be a happy one. But regardless, help others by sharing what your head and heart have learned.

I guess the ending of this book is the best place to say this. My wife and I are expecting our first kid, and for me it is the best thing in the world. What I grew up with, and what my mom Joan had to deal with, will never have to be a part of our child's life. All I want is for my sons, or daughters, to have parents, grandparents, cousins, siblings, and an all-around stable family that doesn't have problems--at least not the addiction problems that we write about in this book. At the end of the day that's what counts, being better than the mistakes you have seen, or mistakes that negatively impacted your life. You don't have to live in the past. Always push forward, and remember that someone else out there needs your help to be the best person they can be.

Real life. Real choices...and a real good ending.

Be kind; everyone you meet
is fighting a hard battle.

Plato

Resources

The following national organizations and government agency program websites often provide information, as well as, state and/or local contacts. They are excellent resources for finding answers to your questions, or help in locating service providers.

For questions and local contact information

211 Resource Line
www.211.org or dial 211.

Provides information and contact numbers/sites for resources in your zip code area for basics including food, housing, health care, clothes.

Generations United
www.gu.org

Website contains statistics, extensive information on terms, laws and most recent financial benefit information. Online publications to help grandparents raising grandkids, including those with disabilities, can be downloaded.

Grandfamilies
www.grandfamilies.org

Extremely easy to use website for parenting grandparents giving information on everything from adoption, financial assistance, housing, kinship navigator programs to subsidized guardianship. Navigators are people who can help guide you through government systems and advise what is available in your state/community; a great service but not available everywhere.

RAPP (Relatives As Parents Program)
http://www.brookdalefoundation.net/RAPP/rapplinks.html

The Brookdale foundation has provided funding to start support groups in 44 states plus Washington, DC and Puerto Rico to help grandparents and other relatives who are taking care of a family member's children. RAPP provides education, networking, and contact referrals.

Social service workers, school staff, family doctors, faith organizations (including local churches, synagogues and mosques) are all good resources when needing help, referrals, or local contact information.

Financial Assistance & Other Support Services

AARP
www.aarp.org/quicklink

Helpful links to TANF, SNAP/food stamps, Medicaid/health insurance and other financial assistance programs. By inputting your family information, you can see quickly what programs you may qualify for, and how to apply.

FANF/TANF: Financial/Temporary Assistance for Needy Families helps low-income families and if the household income exceeds limits grandparents may apply on behalf of their grandchild—then only the child's income is considered. Federal money but administered on a state level. Type in the program name on search engine and add state you are applying to for links.

Social Security Office –See Government

The Addicts Mom
www.addictsmom.com

Chat rooms, blogs, and other helpful emotional support (not financial) and information.

Legal Help

Children's Defense Fund (CDF)
www.childrensdefense.org

Publication resource for kinship families facing legal and justice system issues.

Other helpful resources for information or services include your state bar association, caseworker, law schools and support groups.

Medical, Insurance & Education

Children and Adults with Attention-Deficit/Hyperactivity Disorder (CHADD) www.chadd.org

Information and on-line discussion rooms concerning issues and suggestions for those struggling with ADHD.

Early Childhood Technical Assistance Center (ECTAC)
www.ectacenter.org/families.asp

Site provides extensive information on early intervention and preschool programs funded by the federal government. The 'For Families/Para Families' tab includes easy-to-understand information for individuals. Other parts of the site are geared to professionals serving this population.

Family to Family (F2F)
Contact information by state: http://www.fv-ncfpp.org/files/3213/8996/7192/F2FBrochure_01-15-2014-r.pdf.

Assists families with children having special health care needs. Helpful information for navigating health care systems. Provides information, education, training, support and referral services.

InsureKidsNow.gov
http://insurekidsnow.gov or 800.877.543.7669.

Links and information on affordable health care insurance.

Special Needs Alliance
www.specialneedsalliance.org; info@specialneedsalliance.org; 877.572.8472.

A non-profit organization for individuals with disabilities, their families, and professionals. Links for each state with member attorneys who work with government benefits, special trusts, support and other issues including guardianship and powers of attorney.

The ARC
www.thearc.org

Provides links for finding local chapters offering support and services for parents and persons with intellectual and developmental disabilities. Offers general information on a variety of disorders and disabilities.

Government Programs & Services

U S Department of Health & Human Services-Maternal & Child Health
www.mchb.hrsa.gov/index.html or 888.275.4772.
Provides access to the Medicaid child health program for low-income children needing pediatrician and other health provider services.

U S Department of Interior Affairs-Bureau of Indian Affairs (BIA)
www.bia.gov

Site provides, by tribe, the name and contact information for tribal leaders and the BIA servicing office.

SNAP (Supplemental Nutrition Assistance Program)/food stamps.
www.fns.usda.gov/snap/applicant_recipients/apply.htm

Provides links for each state for you to apply and ask questions regarding food assistance.

Social Security
www.ssa.gov or 800.772-1213.

If one of the birthparents is deceased, your child, or grandchild, may be eligible for survivor benefits, and SSI (social security income) is a monthly payment available, again to some children, with disabilities. Worth checking into.

As a last resort to cutting through red tape contact your state legislator or governor or federal Senator (www.senator.gov) or Representative (www.house.gov). The U S switchboard number is 202.224.3121.

Footnotes

1. "Every Kid Needs a Family: Giving Children in the Child Welfare System the Best Chance for Success." Kids Count. 2015. Annie E. Casey Foundation.

2. When you see this font throughout the book— Chad is doing the writing. For the record, the names of his birth parents, and other families who contributed, are fictional unless a last name is given.

3. Trimbeyer, E. Kay. "Adoption and Genetics: Implication for Adoptive Parents". Huff Post Science. January 30, 2014. Accessed February 1, 2014, http://www.huffingtonpost.com/e-kay-trimbeyer/adoption-and-genetics-imp_b_4682667.html.

4. Rehab International. "Crystal Meth Addiction Statistics." Accessed February 3, 2014, http://rehab-international.org/crystal-meth/addiction-statistics/.

5. Sise, Michael, M.D. "Public Health Consequences of Methamphetamine Abusers." Accessed November 26, 2014, www.ncjrs.gov/ondcppubs/publications/drugfact/methconf/appen-b3.html.

6. "Yes, Your Kid is Smoking Pot: What Every Parent Needs to Know." Q & A interview of Ketcham, Katherine. Accessed March 23, 2014, www.empoweringparents.com.

7. "Facts on Alcohol Related Deaths." Accessed March 31, 2012, www.alcohol-facts.net/Facts-On-Alcohol-Related-Deaths.html.

8. "Alcoholism In-Depth Report." Accessed March 28, 2014, www.nytimes.com/health/guides/disease/alcoholism/print/html.

9. Wallace, Kelly. "Being an addict's mom: "It's just a very, very sad place."" August 28, 2014. Accessed January 4, 2015, www.cnn.com/2014/08/26/living/addiction-parents/.

10. Warren, Rick. "You Don't Have to Forget." Daily Hope email. January 26, 2014.

11. Warren, Rick "Requirements of Restored Relationship." January 25, 2014.

12. "Children Living with Substance-Dependent or Substance-Abusing Parents: 2002 to 2007." The NSDUH Report. April 16, 2009. Accessed February 22, 2014, www.Samhsa.gov/data/2k9/SAparents/SAparents.htm.

13. "Are Children of Alcoholics Different?" Alcohol Alert from National Institute on Alcohol Abuse and Alcoholism. July 1990. Retrieved March 30, 2014 from www.niaaa.nih.gov.

14. "The State of America's Children." 2014 Children's Defense Fund.

15. Denizet-Lewis, Benoit. "Away From Home." review To the End of June, by Chris Beam. The New York Times. August 23, 2013, Sunday Book Review.

16. O'Reilly, Bill. "Are You Your Brother's Keeper?" February 26, 2014. www.foxnews.com.

17. Karr-Morse, Robin and Wiley, Meredith S. *(Ghosts from the Nursery: Tracing the Roots of Violence.)* Atlantic Monthly Press, 2013.

18. Sise, Michael M.D. "Public Health Consequences of Methamphetamine Abusers." Accessed November 18, 2014, https://www.ncjrs.gov/ondcppubs/publications/drugfact/methconf/appen-b3.html.

19. Author unknown.

20. "Grandfamilies: A Blueprint for Coordinated Action". Summary of results from November 19, 2013 Convening. Prepared and distributed by Generations United.

21. "Grounds for Involuntary Termination of Parental Rights." Child Welfare Information Gateway. Accessed September 22, 2014, http://www. childwelfare.gov/systemwide/laws_policies/statutes/ groundtermin.

22. Lakeshore Legal Aid. "Grandparents Raising GrandChildren: Common Legal Issues" Accessed September 24, 2014, http://www.michiganlegalaid.org/ library_client/resource.2005-05-29.1117417905892/ file0/at_download.

23. Forman, Gregory S. "Visitation and the alcoholic parent." April 29, 2009. Accessed January 4, 2015, www.gregoryforman.com/blog/2009/04/visitation-and-the-alcoholic-parent/

24. Zenger, Jack and Folkman, Joseph. "The Ideal Praise-to-Criticism Ratio." Harvard Business Review, March 15, 2013. Accessed January 4, 2015, https://hbr. org/2013/03/the-ideal-praise-to-criticism.

25. West, Tony. "Miss America Fights for Kids with Parents in Prison." Philadelphia The Public Record, February 16, 2012.

26. "The Effects of Prison Visitation on Offender Recidivism." November 2011. Accessed August 10, 2014, http://www.doc.state.mn.us/pages/files/large-files/Publications/11-11MNPrisonVisitationStudy.pdf.

27. "Children of Parents in Jail or Prison: Issues Related to Maintaining Contact." Office of Children

Development. Accessed July 26, 2014, http://ocd.pitt.edu/Default.aspx?webPageID=244.

28. Rothrauff, Tanja and reviewed by Roodhouse, Megan and Bowles, Brian. "When a Child's Parent is incarcerated." April 2008. Accessed August 10, 2014, http://extension.missouri.edu/p/GH6202.

29. Warren, Rick. "Shield of Faith: Protection Money Can't Buy." November 21, 2014.

30. Reardon, Christina, MSW, LSW, "Families and Addiction – Surviving the Season of Stress", Social Work Today, Vol. 11 No 6, 2011.

31. Holohan, Meghan. "Smells like nostalgia: Why do scents bring back memories?" July 19, 2012. Retrieved January 5, 2014 from www.nbcnews.com/health/body-odd/smells-nostalgia-why-do-scents-bring-back-memories-f895521.

32. Oher, Michael and Yaeger, Don. *I Beat the Odds.* Penguin Books Ltd, 2011.

33. Olszewski, Lizabeth, "An Insider's Look at the Holidays with Children of Alcoholics," December 2, 2013. Retrieved May 4, 2015 from http://www.phelpssports.com/viewarticle.php?id+10010181.

34. "Caregiver Grief and Bereavement." Reviewed by Melinda Ratini, DO, MS on July 1, 2013. Retrieved December 6, 2014 from www.webmd.com/palliative-care/caregiver-grief-and-bevreavement?page+2PalliativeCareCenter.

35. Ratini. Ibid.

36. Sangwei, Yoland. "Raising Grandchildren Affects Health of Grandparents." March 6, 2010. Accessed August 11, 2014, www.essence.com/2010/03/06/raising-grandchildren-can-affect-health.

37. "The Health and Well-Being of Grandparents Caring for Grandchildren." Today's Research on Aging, December 2011. Accessed August 11, 2014, http://www.prb.org/pdf11/todaysresearchaging23.pdf.

38. Tavernise, Sabrina. "Married Couples Are No Longer a Majority, Census Finds." New York Times, May 26, 2011. Accessed May 7, 2015, http://www.nytimes.com/2011/05/26/us/26marry.html.

39. Kripke, E. "No Rest for the Wicked." 2008 Television series episode Supernatural.

40. Clear, Monique. Compiled by Voice for Adoption in their 2009 Adoptive Family Portrait Project.

41. Written at a time when Brandy and Ryan were still married and both were clean and sober.

42. Gorman, Melanie. "The Selfish Nature of Addiction: Speaking Honestly About Philip Seymour Hoffman." Accessed November 8, 2014, www.huffingtonpost.com/melanie-gorman/the-selfish-nature-of-addiction_b_4769699.html.

43. McIntosh, Helen, LPC, LCADC, CCS, verbal comments May 17, 2013 Multnomah County Grandparents Raising Grandkids Workshop.

44. "Dysfunctional Families: Recognizing and Overcoming Their Effects." Accessed November 15, 2014, www.twu.edu/downloads/counseling/E-5_Dysfunctional_Families_-_Recognizing_and_Overcoming_Their_Effects.pdf.

45. Lehman, James, MSW. "Anger as a Weapon: When Your Child Points "the Gun" at You." Accessed November 13, 2014, www.empoweringparents.com/Anger-as-a-Weapon-When-Your-Child-Points-the-Gun-at-You.php.

46. "How to help a grieving teen." Accessed January 7, 2015, www.dougy.org/grief-resources/how-to-help-a-grieving-teen/.

47. Dougy Center. Ibid.

48. Real first name.

49. Wallace, Kelly. "Being an addict's mom: 'It's just a very, very sad place'." CNN, Accessed May 7, 2015, http://www.cnn.com/2014/08/26/living/addiction-parents/

50. Deborah. "Parents of Addicts, Addictions Affect Families." Accessed December 16, 2014, http://www.healthyplace.com/other-info-/mental-health-newsletter/parents-of-addicts-addictions-affect-families/#addict.

51. Excerpts from Love Isn't a Vaccine, It's a Poison written by Chad his junior year in high school.

52. David, Susan and Congleton, Christina. "Emotional Agility." Harvard Business Review, November 2013. Accessed December 14, 2014, https://hbr.org/2013/11/emotional-agility.

53. David and Congleton. Ibid.

54. Register, Cheri. "Answering Nosy Questions." Adoptive Families, July/August 1994.

55. Bowman, Dana. "As a Mom in Recovery, How Do I Explain My Addiction to My Kids?" Huff Post, Sept 9, 2014.

56. Dickson, Amy. "Ask Amy." Washington Post, February 24, 2011.

57. Larsen, Rick, U S Representative.

58. Epstein, Fred, M.D. and Josh Horwitz. *(If I get to five: What Children Can teach us about Courage and Character.)* New York: Henry Holt and Company LLC, 2003.

59. Walker, Tim. "Closing the Culture Gap". Tomorrow's Teachers, 2011. Accessed February 12, 2015, www.nea.org;home/43098.htm.

60. Reynolds, Susan. "From Humble Beginnings to Presidential Contender, this Grandpa Is Making a Difference". Grand Magazine, Jan/Feb 2015.

61. "Alcohol Use in Pregnancy." Accessed February 18, 2105, http://www.cdc.gov/ncbddd/fasd/alcohol-use.html.

62. "Drug Tests on Mothers' Hair Links Recreational Drug Use to Birth Defects." Science Daily, October 31, 2014. Accessed February 19, 2015, http://www.sciencedaily.com/releases/2014/10/141031150002.htm.

63. "One Hit of Crystal Meth Can Cause Birth Defects." Accessed February 20, 2015, http://alcoholism.about.com/od/meth/ablut050729.htm.

64. "Hope for Families of Addicts." Accessed February 24, 2015, www.terriblackstock.com.

65. "Fetal Alcohol Syndrome." Accessed February 23, 2013, https://www.ctclearinghouse.org/topics/topic.asp?TopicID+53.

66. Tull, Matthew, PhD. "The Benefits of Exercise for People with PTSD." Accessed February 24, 201, http://ptsd.about.com/od/ptsdandyourhealth/a/ExerciseandPTSD.htm.

67. "The Difference between an IFSP and an IEP." Accessed February 25, 2015, http://www.

mychildwithoutlimits.org/plan/early-intervention/ifsp-iep-comparison/.

68. "Sharp Rise in Use of Childhood Psychiatric Drugs Stirs Concern." Accessed February 25, 2015, http://www.livescience.com/35390-children-psychiatric-medication-over-prescribed-110114.html.

69. Ensroth, Ken M.D. "Ask an Expert: Should I put my child on ADHD medication?" Accessed November 10, 2014, http://attentiondeficit-add-adhd.com/adhd-connors-test.htm.

70. Childrers, Linda. "You, Me, and ADHD." Neurology Now, February/March 2011.

71. Shen, Aviva. "Stop 'Over-Criminalizing' Misbehaving Students." Accessed April 22, 2015, http://thinkprogress. org/justice/2013/03/07/1682141/texas-chief-justice-stop-over-criminalizing-misbehaving-students/.

72. Boyle, Joseph R. PhD. "Enhancing the Note-Taking Skills of Students with Mild Disabilities." Accessed February 25, 2015, http://www.ldonline.org/articlee/ Enhancing_the_Note-Taking_Skills_of_Students_with_ Mild_Disabilities.

73. Accessed March 10, 2015 http://fox6now. com/2015/02/26/touching-groom-reads-vows-to-his-brides-daughter-brings-everyone-to-tears.

74. "U.S. girls are hitting puberty earlier, and earlier, and childhood obesity may be a culprit: Study". NY Daily News.com, November 4, 2013.

75. "Advertising to Children and Teens: Current Practices." Download January 28, 2014 from https://www. commonsensemedia.org/research/advertising-to-children-and-teens-current-practices.

76. "What happens to 'cool' kids? New study sheds light." Science Daily, June 12, 2014.

77. Gettman, Joani MSW. *(A Survival Guide to Parenting Teens.)* New York: Amacom, 2014.

78. Madison, Amber. "When Social-Media Companies Censor Sex Education." The Atlantic, March 4, 2015.

79. Duin, Steve. "And they say Roosevelt is a failing school." The Oregonian/OregonLive.com August 25, 2010. Accessed April 2, 2015, http:www.oregonlive. com/news/oregionian/steve_duin/index.ssf/2010/08/ and_they_say_roosevelt_is_a_fa.html.

Index

Abductions   63, 73-74
Abuse   10, 21, 27-29, 162
ADHD/ADD—See Attention Deficit
Addicts /addictions   7, 12, 16-25, 63, 107-108, 113-114, 181-182
Adoption   13, 29, 32, 37, 56-57
Al-Anon/Alateen   20
Alcoholics 18-25, 28, 60, 63, 108, 113-114, 163-164
Alcoholics Anonymous (AA)   117, 123
Anger   23, 91, 95, 149, 157
Attention Deficit/ Hyperactivity Disorder   150-151
Attitudes 20, 23, 86-87, 90, 97, 101-106, 122-128
Attorneys   22-23, 34-59, 60
Birth Defects   26, 29, 59, 148
Boundaries 79, 98
Caseworkers   9-10, 35, 61, 67
Co-dependency   33
Consequences   27, 34, 92, 98
Coping skills   20, 108, 114, 132-147
Counseling   20, 33, 70, 107-119, 162
Courts   32-33, 35, 40-45, 61
Custody   32, 34-45
Cyber sex and bullying   168-169
Depression   101-102, 149
Disorders & Special Needs   54, 148-162
Divorce   22-23, 43, 51
Drug Users—See Addicts
Drugs-illegal   18, 32, 148, 173-174
Drugs-prescription 55, 83, 156
Emotions   13, 23-25, 54-55, 57, 74, 76-77, 81, 92-96, 103-105, 108-109, 114, 122-147
Enabling   12, 22, 33
Estate Planning   49-59
Family Trees/Projects   102, 141-147
Fathers   27, 30, 164

Feelings—see Emotions
Fetal Alcohol Syndrome   26, 150-152
Finances   38, 47, 51-52
Forgiveness 24-25, 180
Foster Care   27, 108, 131, 163
Fun/Joy   65, 87-90, 105-106, 131
Gangs   28
Government Programs 47, 51, 56
Grandparents 36-37, 43, 47, 56-58, 62, 97-106
Grief   54, 92, 95, 118-120
Guardianship   34-37, 45, 50, 53-54
Guilt   75, 86
Holidays   86-96
Incarceration—see Prison and Jails
Individual Education Plans (IEP)   56, 155-156, 162
Lawyers--See attorneys
Media   21, 133
Mental Health-see Counseling
Native American Rights   48
Oppositional Defiant Disorder (ODD)   152
Parenting   25, 27, 50, 97-100, 116, 162, 163-175
Parental Rights   34, 36, 38, 50, 74
Police   21, 108
Post Traumatic Stress Syndrome   11, 27, 38, 109, 153-154,
Prisons/Jails   76-85
Psychological Parent   10, 46
Reactive Attachment Disorder (RAD)   154-155
Recovery/Rehab   18, 87, 113-114
Relationships   14, 25, 50, 70-72, 76, 120, 176-181
Resources   36, 47, 59, 82, 109, 183-187
Safe People   45, 73, 108
Safety   21, 52, 63-65, 72-74
School & education   47, 102, 132, 141-147, 157-162, 163-164
Self-Care/Self-Talk -- See Attitudes, also Emotions, also
        Support Systems
Sex   25, 164-169
Sexually Transmitted Diseases   168

Siblings   49-52, 88-90, 99, 124
Social Security – See Government Programs
Suicide   12, 86, 123-125
Support Systems   36, 95
Talking to Kids   12, 58-59, 72-73, 93, 100-104, 125-147
Technology   21, 67-68, 77, 133, 165, 168-170
Teenagers   57, 67, 70-71, 80-82, 98-99, 107, 130-131, 163-175
Tough love   15, 123-125
Tough questions 15, 24, 129-147
Trust   30-31, 46, 68, 130
Values   28, 32, 127, 167
Violence 27, 63, 117, 164
Visitations   38, 56, 60-95
Wills   49-54

CPSIA information can be obtained at www.ICGtesting.com
Printed in the USA
LVOW07s2033280815

451974LV00006B/6/P